DISCARDED

DISCARDED

DEFINITION

DEFINITION

BY

RICHARD ROBINSON
FELLOW OF ORIEL COLLEGE, OXFORD

OXFORD
AT THE CLARENDON PRESS

Upsala College
Library
East Orange, N. J.

Oxford University Press, Amen House, London E.C.4

GLASGOW NEW YORK TORONTO MELBOURNE WELLINGTON
BOMBAY CALCUTTA MADRAS KARACHI LAHORE DACCA
CAPE TOWN SALISBURY NAIROBI IBADAN ACCRA
KUALA LUMPUR HONG KONG

160
R663d

86643

REPRINTED LITHOGRAPHICALLY IN GREAT BRITAIN
AT THE UNIVERSITY PRESS, OXFORD
FROM CORRECTED SHEETS OF THE FIRST EDITION
1954,
REPRINTED BY D. R. HILLMAN & SONS, LTD., FROME
1962

ACKNOWLEDGEMENTS

In preparing this essay on definition I have received private help and encouragement from Professor Stuart M. Brown of the Sage School of Philosophy at Cornell University, and Professor Anthony P. Morse of the Department of Mathematics of the University of California at Berkeley, and at Oxford from Mrs. W. C. Kneale, Mr. W. C. Kneale, Mr. A. D. Woozley, Sir David Ross, and the scholar whose advice the Delegates of the Clarendon Press took in deciding to publish it. Of published writings concerning definition I think I have learnt most from those of Plato, Pascal, and Locke.

ACKNOWLEDGMENTS

CONTENTS

§ 1. What is the Definition of 'Definition'? Here is

a list of some of the most famous answers:

1. Plato gives the following three meanings of the word 'logos':
   - (*a*) Revealing one's thoughts by means of speech.
   - (*b*) When someone asks you what a thing is, being able to answer him by means of the elements of the thing.
   - (*c*) Being able to give some mark by which the thing asked about differs from all things.[1]

2. Aristotle in the *Topics*, I 5, defines 'horos' as: the account of the essence of the thing.

3. Cicero: a certain brief and circumscribed account of the properties of the thing we wish to define.[2]

4. Milton: that which refines the pure essence of things from the circumstance.[3]

5. Spinoza: the true definition of each thing involves nothing and expresses nothing but the nature of the thing defined.[4]

6. Locke: making another understand by Words, what Idea the Term defin'd stands for.[5]

7. Kant: to present the complete, original concept of a thing within the limits of its concept.[6]

8. J. S. Mill: a proposition declaratory of the meaning of a word; namely, either the meaning which it bears in common acceptation, or that which the speaker or writer, for the particular purposes of his discourse, intends to annex to it.

9. Whitehead and Russell: a declaration that a certain newly introduced symbol . . . is to mean the same as a certain other combination of symbols of which the meaning is already known.[7]

10. Wittgenstein: Definitions are rules for the translation of one language into another.[8]

---

[1] *Theaetetus*, 206c–7a, 208c.

[2] *De Oratore*, I 42, 189. There is another definition of definition in *Ad Herennium*, IV 25, 35.   [3] *Works* (1851), IV 168.

[4] *Ethics*, I, prop. 8, n. 2.   [5] *Essay*, III. iii. 10.

[6] *Critique of Pure Reason*, A 727, tr. N. K. Smith.

[7] *Principia Mathematica*, 2nd ed., p. 11.   [8] *Tractatus*, 3. 343.

11. Carnap: a rule for mutual transformation of words in the same language.[1]

12. *Oxford English Dictionary*: to state exactly what (a thing) is: to set forth or explain the essential nature of. . . .

> b: to set forth or explain what (a word or expression) means; to declare the signification of (a word). (Part of the article on 'define'.)

Finally we occasionally hear it asserted that:

13. Definition is indefinable. (This may be defended on the ground that 'you cannot define anything until you already understand defining'.)

§ 2. Should a Definition be Brief? That a definition should be brief is included in Cicero's definition of definition quoted above. It is implied in Aristotle's *Topics* (VI 3); and is undoubtedly a very strong and persistent feeling. Yet the contrary view is also often held. Long and laborious processes of definition often occur. E. J. Nelson's definition of entailment takes more than a page to develop.[2] Dewey regarded the whole of his *Logic* as a direct or indirect expansion of his definition of inquiry (104–5). Santayana regarded the definition of beauty as occupying the whole of his book, *The Sense of Beauty* (see below, chapter V, § 7).

§ 3. Should Definitions come at the Beginning or at the End? In mathematical and physical works definitions of terms are most often found at the beginning of that portion of the work which uses these terms; and it seems that a term that needs definition must need it before, not after, it is discussed. On the other hand, the opposite view is frequently held. It is said to have been Goethe's view.[3] It is certainly the view of E. F. Carritt in his *Theory of Beauty*, pp. 2–3: 'It would then be an absurdity to begin with a definition of beauty. To attain that is the object of our inquiry; and even in its proper place the definition would owe any value it possessed to the process by which it had been produced.' J. S. Mill's chapter on justice at the end of his *Utilitarianism*

---

[1] *The Unity of Science*, tr. Max Black, p. 39.
[2] *Mind*, 1930, pp. 443–5.
[3] Fritz Mauthner, *Beiträge zu einer Kritik der Sprache*, III 299.

does not lay down the definition of justice at the beginning but methodically seeks it. Frank Knight has a long, slow approach to a definition of freedom in *Ethics* LII; for example, 'two essential steps by way of analysis and in the direction of sound definition can be made at once in general terms' (91). Often enough both views are stated or implied by the same man, without any suggestion that they need reconciling. For example, many of those who maintain that definition should come at the end probably have in mind those dialogues of Plato which consist in the gradual approach toward a definition. In most of those works the definition is never achieved at all; but if it had been found it would have been found at the end of the dialogue, and the implication of the whole procedure seems to be that definitions cannot be dogmatically asserted at the beginning but must be laboriously sought for in a procedure that takes a long time and indeed constitutes the meat of the work. Yet this same Plato lays it down in the *Phaedrus* that a speech should start with a definition to show what it is about; and this doctrine became a commonplace of the ancient rhetoricians and dialecticians.[1] Spinoza, writing his *Ethics* 'in the geometrical manner', puts definitions at the beginnings of the parts. Yet he collected his definitions of the passions at the end of his derivation of them, not at the beginning. Kant, however, reconciles the two views by distinguishing different sorts of definition.

§ 4. **Are there Indefinables?** Indefinability is constantly being asserted. 'It is logically necessary that some things should be indefinable', wrote A. C. Ewing in *Mind*.[2] Good is indefinable according to G. E. Moore's *Principia Ethica*. 'All' and 'assertion' appear to be indefinable symbols in the view of Dubislav.[3] Poetry is indefinable according to A. E. Housman.[4] Religion is indefinable according to C. C. J. Webb.[5] Quality is indefinable according to S. C. Pepper.[6] According to Tarski, 'truth' is indefinable in common speech, definable in 'poor' constructed languages, and inde-

---

[1] Prantl, *Geschichte der Logik*, usw., I 649.
[2] 1944, p. 79.   [3] *Die Definition*, pp. 61–4.
[4] *The Name and Nature of Poetry*, p. 47.
[5] *Problems in the Relations of God and Man*, introduction.
[6] *Aesthetic Quality*, p. 21.

finable in 'rich' constructed languages.[1] Plato's *Theaetetus*
(201E) contains the earliest surviving version of the doctrine
that 'the primeval letters or elements out of which you and I
and all other things are compounded have no logos'. The
doctrine has been common ever since; for example, it is in
the Port-Royal logic. Locke regarded himself as the first
person to inquire which are the indefinable words.[2] J. S. Mill
held that proper names are indefinable because they are
meaningless, and the names of the simple feelings are
indefinable because the simple feelings are unanalysable.[3]
To Bertrand Russell, writing on *The Philosophy of Leibniz*, it
was an 'obvious truth' that 'we should incur a vicious circle
if we did not admit some indefinable ideas';[4] in the *Introduction to Mathematical Philosophy* he weakened the doctrine to
the extent of being sure only that 'human knowledge must
always be content to accept some terms as intelligible without
definition, in order to have a starting point for its definitions.
[It remains uncertain whether] there must be terms which
are *incapable* of definition' (3–4). But in recent years indefinability has also been often denied. Cohen and Nagel
wrote: 'That there must be undefined terms is clear from any
attempt to define a term. . . . Nevertheless, it is a mistake to
suppose that there are *intrinsically* undefinable terms.'[5] And
W. E. Johnson: 'The problem of definition, it is clear, must
extend to *any* word, however it may be classified by
grammar.'[6]

§ 5. **Have Definitions a Truthvalue?** The search for
definitions in Plato's dialogues is represented as a search
for a certain kind of true statement, and when proposed
definitions are rejected it is usually because they are held
to be false statements. But to-day it is often maintained
that a definition cannot be either true or false, because it is
not a statement but rather a command, not a proposition
but a proposal.

§ 6. **Should Definitions be Tautologies?** Each side of
this contradiction is often asserted. Davidson in his book on
definition writes: 'Avoid tautology . . . the great pitfall of

---

[1] In *Studia Philosophica*, I (Lwow, 1935) 266.   [2] *Essay*, III. iv. 4.
[3] *A System of Logic*, I viii, §§ 1, 2.   [4] 2nd ed., p. 18.
[5] *Introduction to Logic*, &c. (1936), p. 142.   [6] *Logic*, I 103.

lexical definers' (62). This view is embodied in the immensely common rule that a definition should not contain the name to be defined or any synonym for it. On the other side we have, for example, Fritz Mauthner and Louis MacNeice:[1]

> In the beginning and in the end the only decent
> Definition is tautology: man is man,
> Woman woman, and tree tree, and world world,
> Slippery, self-contained; catch as catch can.

§ 7. Is Definition a Useful Procedure or not? Some declare that it is essential to define one's terms, and discussion with undefined terms is useless. Milton held that 'then only we know certainly, when we can define', and he based conclusions about the morality of divorce on a definition of marriage.[2] Refusing to give explanations of one's meaning is the sixth abuse of language according to Locke. Tarski hoped 'that languages with specified structure could finally replace everyday language in scientific discourse'.[3]

Others belittle the use of defining, or even explicitly refuse to define their terms, on the ground that a defined term fails to grasp the reality. R. A. Vaughan made one of his characters speak contemptuously of the 'poor definition-cutter, with his logical scissors'.[4] 'Nothing new can ever be learned by analyzing definitions', writes Peirce. 'Nevertheless, our existing beliefs can be set in order by this process, and order is an essential element of intellectual economy, as of every other' (V 392). A thoroughly contemptuous account of definition is to be found in Fritz Mauthner's Beiträge zu einer Kritik der Sprache (III 299–310). 'I have no great opinion', wrote Edmund Burke, 'of a definition, the celebrated remedy for the cure of [uncertainty and confusion]. For when we define, we seem in danger of circumscribing nature within the bounds of our own notions.'[5] He was feeling, I think, for the doctrine that a mathematically rigid insistence on using your words only in strictly defined senses will confine your possible discourse to the narrow sphere of mathematics, and prevent you, for example, from ever

[1] *Plant and Phantom*, 1941, p. 81.   [2] *Works* (1851), IV 168.
[3] In *Philosophy and Phenomenological Research*, IV 347.
[4] *Hours with the Mystics* (2nd ed., 1860), I 209.
[5] *The Sublime and Beautiful*, Introduction.

talking politics or history. 'We are often deprived', wrote
I. A. Richards, 'of very useful thoughts merely because the
words which might express them are being temporarily
preempted by other meanings', and he therefore urges us
to use words in many senses.[1] Whitehead has written that
'insistence on hardheaded clarity issues from sentimental
feeling, as it were a mist, cloaking the perplexities of fact.
Insistence on clarity at all costs is based on sheer superstition
as to the mode in which human intelligence functions.'[2]

§ 8. **What are the Species of Definition?**   Into what
sorts does it divide? The nature of the problem here may
be suggested by making a list of names for sorts of definition
found in good writers.

1. Real definition (most textbooks).
2. Nominal definition (most textbooks).
3. Extensive definition (Keynes).
4. Ostensive definition (W. E. Johnson).
5. Analytic definition (W. E. Johnson).
6. Synthetic definition (W. E. Johnson).
7. Equational definition (S. C. Pepper).
8. Descriptive definition (S. C. Pepper).
9. Operational definition (Bridgman).
10. Genetic definition (J. E. Creighton).
11. Definition in use (Whitehead and Russell).
12. Denotative definition (Levi and Frye).
13. Connotative definition (Levi and Frye).
14. Implicit definition (Gergonne).
15. Co-ordinating definition (Reichenbach).
16. Persuasive definition (Stevenson).
17. Successive definition (Lenzen).
18. Definition by description (Lewis).

§ 9. **To What Sort of Entity does Definition apply?**
Do we define things, or words, or concepts? In other words, are
we to be *realists*, or *nominalists*, or *conceptualists*, about
definition?

When the notion of definition was invented by Socrates
and Plato, only 'real definition' was thought of. That is, it
was always *res* or things that required definition, never

[1] *Interpretation in Teaching*, p. 384.   [2] *Adventures of Ideas*, p. 91.

nomina or words or concepts. Definition was in fact, according to Plato, the end of the process of getting to know the most real things there are, which he called Forms or Ideas. Thus a correct statement of the definition of the Good would be an expression of the most important kind of knowledge or insight a man could possibly have.

Aristotle, though in many respects he carried logic far beyond the point to which Plato had brought it, made little or no advance with regard to the question whether we define things or words or concepts. It is possible to point to a few sentences in which he regards the definiendum as a word and not a thing. But the idea had no great effect on him. He defines definition as 'the account of the essence of the *thing*'; and most of his long discussions of definition deal with problems that arise out of this thoroughly realist point of view. For example, when we have a true account of the essence of a thing, then, he thought, we have the most important kind of knowledge anybody could want. It therefore becomes urgent to discover how we can tell whether any given definition is true or false. Now the normal way of ascertaining whether a proposition is true or false is, according to Aristotle, to submit it to the process of 'demonstration', that is, of syllogistic inference from selfevident principles, as he explains in his *Prior Analytics* and in the first book of his *Posterior Analytics*. The way to make sure that you had the correct definition would be, therefore, to 'demonstrate' it. But *can* definitions be demonstrated? On the contrary, must not definition be already given, as a selfevident principle, before any demonstration of anything can begin? Aristotle wrestles with this problem in the first thirteen chapters of the second book of his *Posterior Analytics*; and their incredible obscurity is a measure of its difficulty to him. Similarly, the extreme difficulty of his *Metaphysics Z* is due to its being about the question, What is this *essence* which it is the function of a definition to give?, a question which again presupposes that definition is of things, not words or concepts.

The habit of regarding definition as primarily or exclusively about things has been common ever since. Spinoza wrote that 'the true definition of each thing involves nothing

and expresses nothing but the nature of the thing defined'.[1]
Joseph wrote that 'definitions . . . are not really of names'.[2]

This view is losing its predominance, however. For centuries now most conventional accounts of definition have recognized two sorts: real and nominal. Persons who tend to reject Aristotle have inclined towards the other extreme that definition is always of words. Pascal on *The Spirit of Geometry* did not deny the occurrence of real definition, but confined his attention to the nominal species. Locke and J. S. Mill, as we have seen, flatly defined definition so that it had to be of words and not of things. Stebbing wrote that 'definition is always of symbols, verbal or otherwise'.[3]

A third habit of talking, according to which that which is defined is neither a word nor a thing but a concept, has arisen and maintained itself, modestly in most countries, luxuriantly in Germany. It is expressed, for example, in Kant's statement that to define is 'to present the complete, original concept of a thing within the limits of its concept'. It is essential to Heinrich Rickert's essay on definition. It seems, however, rarely to attain the rank of being listed alongside the real and the nominal as a third sort of definition.

How are we to interpret the extreme views, which admit only one sort of definition? When a man says that 'all definition is nominal (or real, or conceptual), and there is no other kind', what are we to take him as meaning? There seem to be three possible interpretations:

1. When a man says that 'all definition is nominal', he might perhaps mean that the word 'definition' never has, as a matter of past usage, been applied to any process that was not a process concerning words. If so, he would be making an historical statement about actual past usage. It is already clear that his statement, if meant in this sense, would be false. Hundreds of persons have in the past applied the word 'definition' to processes and statements that were not about words. Our list of definitions of definition shows that, while some good writers have used the word 'definition' to refer to a process dealing with words (Locke, Mill), other

---

[1] *Ethics*, I, prop. 8, n. 2.
[2] *An Introduction to Logic*, 2nd ed., p. 82.
[3] *A Modern Introduction to Logic*, 2nd ed., p. 439.

good writers have used it to refer to a process dealing with things (Aristotle, Milton), and others to a process dealing with concepts (Kant). Mill's statement that 'no definition is ever intended to "explain and unfold the nature of a thing" '[1] would be grossly false if taken as an account of the past usage of the word.

2. The nominalist might reply as follows: 'I do not deny that Aristotle *thought* he was talking about a definition of things, and Kant *thought* he was talking about a definition of concepts. But I wish to maintain that there are no such occurrences as definition of things and definition of concepts, so that if Aristotle and Kant thought that these things really happened or could happen they were mistaken. I further suggest that what led them into those mistakes was a confused intuition of something that really can happen, namely nominal definition.' On this interpretation the statement that 'all definition is nominal' is not about usages at all. It is a statement about human knowledge, its nature and possibilities, to the effect that what men have meant by the phrase 'nominal definition' is something that can occur, but what men have meant by the phrases 'real definition' and 'conceptual definition' are things that cannot occur, mistaken figments of the mind, imperfect and distorting efforts to grasp that genuine occurrence whose name is 'nominal definition'.

On this second interpretation the question whether any one of the extreme views is true is by no means so easy as on the first interpretation. All that is obvious is that not more than one of them can be true. It cannot be true, for example, both that all definition is of words and that all definition is of things. Further discussion of the question is unsuitable for an introductory chapter.

3. A third interpretation of the extreme views would be that they are proposals for future usage. For example, that, when Stebbing wrote that definition is always of symbols, she meant to propose that in future we should decline to apply the word 'definition' to any operation that was not about symbols; while, when Joseph wrote that definitions are not really of names, he was trying to persuade us, for example, to give up calling the articles in the dictionary 'definitions'.

[1] *A System of Logic*, I 163.

The propriety of such proposals would obviously depend on our answer to the questions raised by the second interpretation, namely, whether there is such a thing as the real definition that Aristotle believed in, whether there is such a thing as the conceptual definition that Kant believed in, and whether there is such a thing as the nominal definition that Locke believed in. It is therefore again a matter that an introductory chapter can only introduce and not decide.

So much for controversies about definition.

WORD-THING DEFINITION

§ 1. Meanings of the Word 'Definition'. The usage of
the word 'definition' varies in numerous dimensions, and one
of these dimensions will now be noticed. The word sometimes refers to a certain human activity. This activity is
usually mediated by a sentence, either uttered by the definer
or imagined in his mind. Men have applied the word 'definition' more often to the sentence than to the mental activity
which the sentence makes possible. They have given the
name 'definition' to the sentence 'God is the supreme spirit'
rather than to the activity of realizing that God is the supreme
spirit. Besides being applied to the activity and to the
sentence, the word 'definition' is applied, thirdly, to the
meaning of the sentence. Fourthly and fifthly, the word is
often confined to a certain part of the sentence or of its
meaning, namely, the predicative part. On this usage in the
sentence 'God is the supreme spirit' the definition is only the
last three words or their meaning. Sixthly, the word 'definition' often carries one of the meanings of the word 'sense'.
Thus when I. A. Richards advises us to use many definitions
of the same term,[1] he is advising us to use words in several
senses without defining the senses. Seventhly, the words
'define' and 'definition' are sometimes used to mean merely
any pithy saying of the form 'X is ———'.

Along this dimension, then, we have the following seven
senses of the word 'definition':

1. A certain human activity, intellectual in character.
2. The sentence which mediates or expresses this activity.
3. The meaning of this sentence.
4. The predicative part of the sentence.
5. The meaning of the predicative part of the sentence.
6. A sense of a word.
7. A pithy saying of the form 'X is ———'.

I venture to suggest that the sixth sense is bad and should
be avoided. It is a meaning that appears to be well provided

[1] *Interpretation in Teaching.*

for by the word 'sense', and it excludes something that is characteristic of the preceding five senses, namely, the *secondary* symbolic activity of talking about one's symbolizations. The word 'definition' is not wanted to describe anything in the *primary* activity of using symbols. It is wanted to describe some subsequent process that reflects on the use of symbols.

Also undesirable is the use of the words 'definition' and 'define' to refer merely to a pithy saying, as when Bismarck is said to have 'defined' politics as the art of the possible, and Sandburg to have 'defined' slang as language which takes off its coat, spits on its hands, and goes to work.[1] Each of the first five senses has its advantage and may often be the best. However, there exists a more precise word for the fourth and fifth. The predicative part of the sentence, or its meaning, is known as the 'definiens', in contrast to the subject, which is known as the 'definiendum'. And it is usually better to keep to this word for these two senses when it is certain that one's readers understand them, for example, to write 'the definiens must be equivalent to the definiendum', and not 'the definition must be equivalent to what it defines'.

The most important of these five senses is the first, definition as an intellectual activity. It is the fount of all the other four. Definition is a human activity before it is anything else. It would be a mistake to concentrate on the sentence instead of the activity, because the same sentence may express very different sorts of defining activity. The sentence 'Her name is Joan', uttered by the mother of a new born child, may be the first arbitrary assignment of a name. But, uttered by a friend ten years later, it is an historical report of actual usage or of that past assignment. If we clung to the sentence and refused to consider the mental state of the namer or definer, we should be examining a hollow shell and overlooking important differences.

The above insistence on the mental state of the definer stamps this essay as what many logicians disapprovingly call 'psychological'. For example, Professor A. J. Ayer, in *Language, Truth, and Logic*, wrote that 'the discussion of psychological questions is out of place in a philosophical

[1] *Life*, 15 Dec. 1941, p. 89.

enquiry' (187), and rebuked 'the traditional logic' for 'introducing irrelevant psychological questions' (107); and this
attitude is very common. But what a mysterious taboo it is!
Does it mean that, if an author promises to be strictly philosophical in the sense of introducing no psychology into his
book, then he should keep his promise and introduce no
psychology? But there seems no reason to make such a
promise, and certainly none is made in this work. Does it
mean that those who share this view are not interested in
psychology? Obviously it does not, for there would be no
point in publishing such limitedness if it existed. Does it
mean that anyone who utters both philosophical and psychological statements in the same chapter will be thereby led
into more error than truth? This seems the most likely
interpretation. But, if this is the meaning, it requires
elaboration and defence. Is there not a proper place for the
combination of logic and psychology, as there is for the
combination of mathematics and physics? It is important
that pure logic and pure psychology should not be confused,
but is it not also important that we should study the ground
where they touch? It is a psychological fact that the human
mind thinks, and thinks among other things about logical
matters including definitions; and the adequate investigation
of this must be both psychological and logical.

It is a peculiar feature of learned writings in the last fifty
years that a great deal of space is spent in arguing just what
does and does not fall under the head of 'logic', or 'psychology', or 'sociology', or 'economics', or 'political science'.
To mention another example, Dr. Leslie White has written:
'The duty and task of giving an account of the organic basis
of symbolizing does not fall within the province of the
sociologist or the cultural anthropologist. On the contrary,
he should scrupulously exclude it as irrelevant to his problems
and interests; to introduce it would bring only confusion.'
The idea that any man should scrupulously exclude any field
of knowledge from his thoughts! The more defensible
doctrine, which Dr. White probably meant to express here,
is that certain particular questions about symbolizing, which
he only vaguely indicates as being sociological or anthropo-
logical, are better solved if we for the time being put aside

all thoughts about the organic basis of symbolizing. It is true that success in the study of one particular problem sometimes comes by resolutely forgetting other matters for the moment. It is also true that it sometimes comes by the opposite procedure. It is true that some of this insistence on sharp divisions between sciences arises out of the valuable effort to get clear about the essence of the new ways of thinking that have recently arisen in profusion. It is also true that some of it is an unconscious attempt to justify the narrowness of one's own interests and excuse one from examining borderline matters which are relevant but distasteful. Some of it is even merely a way of claiming the exclusive right to teach a certain subject-matter in the universities.

§ 2. The Fundamental Classification of Definitions. Let us distinguish between the *purpose* and the *method* of a definition. The purpose of a definition is what it is trying to do; and the method is the means which it adopts to achieve its purpose. Different definitions have different purposes; and they achieve them by different methods. We shall be much clearer if we know which of the names of a special sort of definition (above, p. 7) are names of a *purpose* of definition, which are names of a *method*, and which are names of a specific purpose achieved by a specific method. For example, 'nominal definition' is the name of a purpose, the purpose of explaining the meaning of a word; but 'ostensive definition' is the name of a method, the method that makes use of pointing or physical introduction. In order to achieve a nominal definition, one can use the ostensive method, or one can use some other method.

It would ·be an error to co-ordinate a purpose with a method, just as it would be an error to list together tables and chairs and sawing and planing, because sawing and planing are *methods* of carpentry, but tables and chairs are *purposes* of carpentry. Carnap made this error by co-ordinating nominal definition with ostensive definition in the following passage:

'A definition is a rule for mutual transformation of words in the same language. This is true both of so-called nominal definitions (e.g. "Elephant" = animal with such and such distinguishing characteristics) and also, a fact usually forgotten, for so-called ostensive definitions (e.g. "Elephant" = animal of the same kind as the animal in this or that position in space-time); both definitions are translations of words.'[1]

The error was in this case only superficial; for what Carnap really had in mind when he wrote 'so-called nominal definitions' was the analytic method of nominal definition; and the analytic method of nominal definition may properly be contrasted with the ostensive method of nominal definition. But serious further errors have often flowed from this failure to distinguish when one is talking about a purpose of definition and when about a method. We must have not one but two lists of sorts of definition, one of the purposes and one of the methods.

I now proceed to the classification of the purposes of definition. The supreme division here is into *nominal and real definition*, the oldest division of definitions. The purpose of nominal definition is something to do with *nomina* or words or signs or symbols. I cannot describe it accurately at this stage, and later it will become clear from its subdivisions; but roughly the purpose of nominal definition is to report or establish the meaning of a symbol. The purpose of real definition, on the other hand, is nothing to do with *nomina* or words or signs or symbols. It is something to do with *res* or things. The things may happen to be symbols; but that is only because they may be any things, and symbols are things; usually they are not symbols. Real definition is concerned with things in general; but nominal definition is concerned only with a peculiar sort of thing, namely, symbols.

Real and nominal definition are *proximate* purposes of definition. There may be any number and any sort of *ulterior* purposes, beyond the proximate purpose. A definition may be performed with the ultimate aim of teaching someone cookery, or overthrowing a government, or reaching Mars. But the immediate purpose, the purpose that makes us call the activity a 'definition', is one of these two.

I shall not subdivide real definition until Chapter VI. I now subdivide nominal definition into *word-word and word-thing definition*. The purpose of all nominal definition being to report or establish the meaning of a word or symbol,

[1] *The Unity of Science*, tr. by Max Black. 1934, p. 39.

word-word definition does this in the form of saying that one word means the same as another word, and word-thing does it in the form of saying that a word means a certain thing. If, for example, someone tells you that the German word 'rot' means the same as the French word 'rouge', while you remain ignorant what either of these words refers to, that is a word-word definition. If, on the other hand, he points to the cover of a book on his shelves and says that the German word 'rot' means that colour, he gives you a word-thing definition. Word-word definition correlates a word to another word, as having the same meaning. Word-thing definition correlates a word to a thing, as meaning that thing.

Word-thing definition is correlating a word to a thing. Therefore, to communicate a word-thing definition to my friend I must draw his attention both to the word and to the thing. How do I do that? Drawing his attention to the word is very simple; I merely utter the word, which I can always do. But how do I draw his attention to the thing? I cannot utter things, and I cannot always produce the thing I want. Here arises a fact that is liable to confuse us. In order to complete my word-thing definition, I usually draw my friend's attention to the thing by using some other word or words with which he is already familiar. For instance, I tell him what thing the German word 'rot' means by saying ' "rot" means red'. But that does not imply that after all I have not given him a word-thing definition but a word-word defini-tion. I have given him a word-thing definition, because I have directed his attention to a certain thing, and told him that 'rot' is a name of that thing. By 'word-thing' definition I mean correlating a word to a thing, *however you do it*, and whether or not you introduce the thing by means of other words. The *method* by which you proceed does not alter the *purpose*, which is to correlate a word to a thing.

Every word-word definition necessarily implies a word-thing definition to those hearers who know the meaning of one of the words. If you say 'the word "rot" fulfils the same function in the German language as the word "rouge" in the French language', that is a word-word definition; but, to those of your hearers who know what either 'rot' or 'rouge' means, it implies a word-thing definition. A huge number of nominal definitions are adequate vehicles for both the word-word and the word-thing purpose. We must not allow this frequent coincidence of the two purposes to prevent us from seeing that they are two, not one. It is one enterprise to point out that two names are equivalent; it is another enterprise to point out that a certain sign is a name of a certain thing. And, though there are many utterances which achieve both these purposes at once, there are also many utterances which achieve only one of them.

We now have three purposes of definition, namely, real definition and the two sorts of nominal definition. If we call real definition 'thing-thing' definition, we can list these three purposes as follows:

1. Word-word, i.e. the first sort of nominal definition.
2. Word-thing, i.e. the second sort of nominal definition.
3. Thing-thing, i.e. real definition.

It is important to notice that some people ignore the possibility of word-thing definition, and write as if all definition were either word-word or thing-thing. Here is a recent example of such writing:

'One is tempted to ask what the word *useful* may mean in this connection. . . . Are we to be given mere synonyms and told that utility means the same as such and such a word in such and such a language, as for instance *utile* in Latin? But does not such an answer presuppose that there is a *real* meaning common to all these words? Would anyone ever look up a word in a dictionary if he thought that no word ever meant anything except other *words*? . . . One may pardon the reader who prefers even the Platonic search for essences, in spite of its difficulties, to the apparently complete scepticism and nominalism of the "twentieth century" alternative.'

This author sees nothing between word-word definition (as in ' "utile" and "useful" are equivalent words') and thing-thing definition (as in the Platonic search for essences). Since he furthermore considers word-word definition a very useless and unnecessary enterprise, he is left with thing-thing definition as the only valuable kind. He tends to argue thus: 'Word-word definition is futile; therefore the only important kind of definition is thing-thing definition.' But this is an error, because it overlooks the possibility of word-thing definition, the act of connecting a certain word to a certain thing.

This author uses the word 'nominalism', which is opposed to the word 'realism'. But, since we are dealing here with *three* sorts of definition, it is confusing to apply language which recognizes a division into *two* only. If it is 'nominalism' to believe in word-word definition, and 'realism' to believe in thing-thing definition, what is it to believe in word-thing definition?

I personally believe that all three kinds of definition, word-word, word-thing, and thing-thing, are possible events, and occur from time to time, and have their value; but thing-thing definition had better be called by some other name than 'definition'. I discuss word-thing definition in Chapters II, III, IV, and V, and thing-thing definition in Chapter VI. I do not discuss word-word definition; and I agree with the 'realists' that its importance is slight.

Finally, I subdivide word-thing definition into *lexical and stipulative definition*. Here by 'lexical definition' I mean reporting the customary or dictionary meaning of a word, and by 'stipulative definition' I mean establishing or announcing or choosing one's own meaning for a word. I deal with lexical definition in Chapter III, and with stipulative definition in Chapter IV.

Definition divided according to Purpose

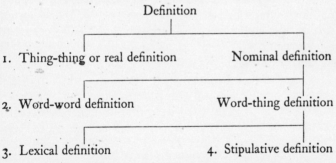

Definition

1. Thing-thing or real definition   Nominal definition

2. Word-word definition   Word-thing definition

3. Lexical definition   4. Stipulative definition

To avoid confusion, it is worth remarking that the phrase 'the distinction between real and nominal definition', which I use to express the belief that definition is a process which can be applied either to things or to words, has sometimes been used in other senses which are not intended here. I will mention, to exclude them, three of these other senses.

1. Perhaps some people mean by 'real as opposed to nominal definition' what I mean by 'lexical as opposed to stipulative word-thing definition'.

2. By 'the distinction between nominal and real definition' has sometimes been meant the distinction between word-word definition and all other kinds. Word-word definition connects a word to other words, and never goes outside the sphere of symbols at all. It merely says that this symbol is equivalent to that symbol. Word-thing definition, on the other hand, goes outside the sphere of symbols because it connects the word to some non-symbolic object which is the meaning of that word. And thing-thing definition is never inside the sphere of symbols at all. If we distinguish the three kinds, word-word, word-thing, and thing-thing, then 'the distinction between nominal and real definition' is sometimes taken to mean the distinction between word-word definition and the other two; but I am taking it to mean the distinction between word-word or word-thing definition on the one hand and thing-thing definition on the other.

3. We define 'regular dodecahedron' to mean a solid bounded by twelve sides which are all regular polygons of the same size and shape, and such a thing is possible. We could define 'regular decahedron' to mean a solid bounded by ten sides which are all regular polygons of the same size and shape, but such a thing is impossible. Leibniz used the words 'nominal' and 'real' to refer to this distinction. By a 'real' definition he meant a word-thing definition where the thing in question is known to be possible. By a 'nominal' definition he meant a word-thing definition where the thing in question is not known to be possible. In this language it is true to say that what mathematicians call an 'existence' proof is or suggests a proof that a certain definition is real.

This and closely similar usages have often occurred since Leibniz. But they do not occur in this essay. In my usage every word-thing definition is a nominal definition, no matter what is known or unknown about the possibility of the thing in question.

§ 3. **The Extent of Word-thing Definition.** By 'word-thing' definition I mean definition that is either lexical or legislative, which is equivalent to any kind of definition whose purpose is either to report or to establish the meaning of a symbol.

The broadest interpretation of word-thing definition would be: any process, whether verbal or otherwise, by which any individual, whether God or angel or man or beast, brings any individual, whether himself or another, to know the meaning of any elementary symbol, whether verbal or other, and if a verbal symbol whether a noun or an adjective or a preposition or any other sort of word. But few people have ever used the word 'definition' in so broad a sense as this, and some have declared much narrower senses to be still too broad. Thus Stebbing wrote that 'we must be careful not to use "definition" so widely that it comes to stand for any process enabling us to learn the application of words. These processes are so different that to call them by the same name leads to confusion.'[1]

The narrowest sense of word-thing definition that has found common acceptance is this: the process in which a human being explains to a different human being the meaning of a general noun by using words that give an analysis of the thing meant. There are seven respects in which this sense is narrower than the former. Five of them narrow the purpose of definition, and two of them narrow the method by which that purpose may be achieved.

1. Definition is here restricted to human beings. This excludes a man teaching a dog the meaning of 'walk', and a dog teaching a man the meaning of one of its gestures, and a dog teaching a dog the meaning of anything.

2. Definition is here restricted to the actions of one human upon another human. This excludes all processes by which a man might bring himself to know the meaning of a word he did not know before, without the intentional help of any second person. Whether it excludes his doing something now to help his own understanding of words five years hence would be a matter for further specification. But, disregarding that complication, we are now confined to events where one human, who already knows the meaning of a symbol, makes it known to a second human who was ignorant of it.

[1] *A Modern Introduction to Logic*, ed. 2, p. 422.

Upsala College

Library

East Orange, N. J.

3. Definition is here restricted to the definition of verbal symbols. This excludes teaching a man the meaning of a signal bonfire.

4. Furthermore, within the sphere of verbal symbols we are now further restricted to nouns. The common word in logical treatises is 'terms'. This includes all sets of words that can take the place of a noun, and perhaps it includes adjectives regarded as more or less nouns. It certainly excludes verbs and adverbs and prepositions and conjunctions.

5. The last of the restrictions which this narrower definition places upon the purposes that may be called 'word-thing' definition is that the defined term must be a general term. Words can be defined only if they are names of something general. On this restriction the explanation of the name of a particular is not definition. To tell a man what 'island' means is definition, but to tell him what 'Mona' means is not.

6. This narrow sense of 'word-thing' definition also restricts the method by which we may achieve our aim. It declares in the first place that we must proceed by using words. Not merely must the symbol defined be a word, as we saw in the three preceding paragraphs, but also the means by which we define it must be words. This excludes teaching a person the meaning of the word 'rectangle' by pointing to a rectangle.

7. Lastly, this narrow sense of 'word-thing' definition demands that the words employed to explain the meaning shall do so by giving an analysis of the thing meant. This excludes defining 'rectangle' as the shape which the pages of a book have.

Some but not all of these limitations are included in John Locke's definition of definition as 'making another understand by words, what Idea the Term defined stands for'. Here we have the first limitation implicitly (he is assuming that this goes on only between humans), the second explicitly ('making another understand'), the third and fourth explicitly ('the Term defined'). He does not demand here the fifth restriction, that the defined term must be a general term. He explicitly demands the sixth restriction when he says 'by words'. He does not here demand the seventh, that the explanatory words shall proceed by giving an analysis of the thing defined.

All of these seven limitations are rejected in the present work, and the phrase 'word-thing definition' is used in the unusually broad sense defined at the beginning of this section. Some of the reasons for this choice will now be briefly indicated.

As to (1), we may believe that among occurrent things humans alone are able to teach and learn the meanings of symbols; but we need a name for the teaching of elementary symbols wherever it occurs.

As to (2), if we restricted 'word-thing' definition to those cases where the teacher and the learner are not the same person we should exclude the most important part of legislative definition, the activity of the thinker in arriving at a new meaning by his own creation.

As to (3), there is no important difference between teaching a man the meaning of the green colour in a traffic-light and teaching him the meaning of the word 'go' in a sentence. If the light corresponds to a sentence, not to a word, at least the mere colour taken by itself corresponds to a word, when we abstract from its position at a crossroads and its direction as referring to a particular entrance. The difference between explaining a word and explaining a sentence is very important; but it is not the same as that between explaining a verbal and a non-verbal symbol. Let us not, therefore, restrict 'word-thing' definition to the explanation of verbal symbols.

4. The further restriction to the explanation of *nouns*, excluding all other grammatical classes of words, seems wholly pointless. A dictionary that confined itself to nouns would be of little use. We need to know the meanings of all words, not merely of nouns.

5. Is there a good reason for restricting 'definition' to the explanation of words meaning a certain class of object? In particular, of words meaning a general object as opposed to proper names, since this is the only distinction which has often been felt to warrant a difference of name? The answer appears to be no. Proper names and general names both have meanings that have to be learnt. When Mill said that

proper names could not be defined because they had no meaning he was using 'meaning' in a narrow sense; for obviously proper names mean something to those who use them, and obviously those who come into a new district or a new society have to learn the meaning of proper names. The explanation of proper names is word-thing definition as much as the explanation of any word.

Then why this persistent reluctance to talk of the 'definition' of the word 'Cicero'? Why does logician after logician repeat the doctrine that proper names are indefinable?

We touch here upon the fundamental reason why most of these restrictions upon the scope of word-thing definition are made and ought not to be made. It is that nominal definition has never yet been adequately distinguished from real definition, so that people are always laying upon nominal definition restrictions that inhere in the nature of real definition but have no relevance to nominal definitions. This is true even of many persons who deny that there is such a thing as real definition. They, too, narrow nominal definition in a way appropriate only to real definition.

The reason why men think there is no definition of names for particular objects is that it is difficult to keep nominal definition distinct from real definition, and there can be no real definition of particular objects but only of general objects. Since the real definition of objects is not clearly distinguished from the nominal definition of names for objects, the impossibility of giving a real definition of particular objects comes to be confusedly thought of as the impossibility of giving a nominal definition of names for particular objects.

This explanation appeals to two facts, or makes two assertions: (*a*) that nominal definition is hard to keep distinct from real definition, and (*b*) that there can be no real definition of particular objects but only of general objects.

(*a*) That nominal definition is hard to keep distinct from real definition. Do we or do we not know what the word 'justice' means? It is not clear. If we do know, Plato's definition of justice is presumably real. If we do not know, it is nominal. And which is J. S. Mill's definition of justice at the end of his *Utilitarianism*? It reads like real definition, but Mill in his *Logic* denied the occurrence of real definition. And is the statement that two is one plus one a real definition of two, or a nominal definition of the word 'two', or neither? Frege was thinking of such statements when he wrote: 'As such the definition of an object really says nothing about the object, but determines the meaning of a sign. After that has occurred, the definition changes itself into a judgement which is about the object and which is also no longer the introduction of the object but on the same footing as other statements about it.'[1] Most words in our own language suggest something to us before we know their precise meanings, and it is hard to say in many instances whether what we are doing is the nominal activity of jettisoning our old vague meaning for the word and taking another, or the real activity of realizing the nature and complexity of what we already mean by the word.

(*b*) That there can be no real definition of particular objects but only of general objects. Every attempt to describe the real nature of Cicero gives an essence that might possibly belong to some other person too; therefore it only gives the essence of some generalized man. We can never mention as the essential nature of some particular object anything but the essential nature of some general object which is a sort to which the particular belongs. It is therefore impossible to give a definition expressing fundamental knowledge of the essential nature of some particular object as other than the essential nature of some general object.

If then real definition is only of general objects, and the real definition of an object is not clearly distinguished from the word-thing definition of the name for that object, it naturally comes to be felt that word-thing definition is possible only of names for general objects, and hence that names for particular objects are indefinable.

6. Is it convenient to refuse to call an explanation of the meaning of a word a 'word-thing definition' unless it proceeds by means of words? Stebbing answered yes, on the ground that the various processes by which the application of words may be taught 'are so different that to call them by the same name leads to confusion'. The greatest difference

---

[1] *Die Grundlagen der Arithmetik*, p. 78.

here is between those processes which proceed by words and those which proceed without them. Since we all begin life knowing the use of no words, our first instruction in them must occur without the aid of words; and the method by which this is done, whatever it is, may perhaps occur in later life also.

Stebbing was right in this, that where there are differences we ought to have distinct names for the different objects, so that we can distinguish and contrast them when desirable. But it does not follow that, if two different objects with two distinct names have also something in common, we ought not to have a third name that covers both of them in virtue of their community. Teaching the use of a word by means of other words, and teaching the use of a word without the use of other words, are distinct as regards their methods, and therefore should be given distinct names when we are distinguishing methods. But they are also identical in their fundamental purpose, which is to teach the use of a word; and there ought to be a name that embraces both of them in virtue of their identity. What more suitable name than 'definitions'? It is very likely that here, too, the reluctance to accord this name to all methods of teaching the meaning of a word is due to the imperfect separation of nominal from real definition, for real definition is an enterprise that is practically impossible without words.

7. All the more must we say that, when the purpose called 'word-thing definition' *is* achieved by means of words, these words may be of any effective sort, and need not necessarily proceed by giving an analysis of the thing meant by the word to be defined. The demand that a word-thing definition proceed by analysing the thing meant by the word, or the still more specific demand that this analysis take the form of genus and difference, is the crowning example of a false limitation imposed on nominal definition through confusing it with real definition. The real definition of an object is an analysis of that object. There is no other way of giving a real definition of an object than by analysing it. (This point will be developed when we come to real definition. Here we can only assert it.) If, therefore, we confuse nominal with real definition, we come to think falsely that there is no other way

of giving a word-thing definition of a word than by analysing the object it stands for. But this limitation is pointless if what we are discussing is the task of explaining the meaning of a word; for, as we shall see, that can be done in several other ways, and sometimes it must be done in other ways. Men have confined the term 'definition' to analytical operations in the case of *words* merely because it had to be confined to analytical operations in the case of *objects*, and they did not clearly distinguish these sorts of definition from each other.

There are interesting cases of persons who repudiate real definition altogether, and yet limit their account of nominal definition in a way that has no ground but the secret survival of real definition in their minds. Thus Stebbing, who maintained that all definition is of symbols, nevertheless limited definition to such explanations of the meaning of a symbol as asserted the equivalence of two expressions; where the defining expression had to contain more symbols than the defined expression. There is no reason for this limitation except the irrelevant one that real definition, being an analysis, will necessarily be expressed in a statement of equivalence whose right-hand side contains more symbols. A similar peculiarity in Locke is described below in the discussion of the synthetic method of word-thing definition. Real definition is a most persistent plant, still growing obscurely even in gardens where it is considered the merest weed.

The phrase 'word-thing definition', then, means in this book any process, whether verbal or otherwise, by which any individual, whether God or angel or man or beast, brings any individual, whether himself or another, to know the meaning of any elementary symbol, whether a word or other, and if a word whether a noun or an adjective or a preposition or any other sort of word.

§ 4. **The Utility of Word-thing Definition.** Some persons consider word-thing definition and the study of word-thing definition worthless enterprises. Such matters, they feel, are merely verbal and give no important knowledge. We should disregard words and give our attention to things.

The following facts tend to show that this view is a mistake. Words are the means to a knowledge of things.

Without them an animal's knowledge is confined to his own unanalysed memories and perceptions of his own experience. Without them there is little analysis, little generalization, and no transmission of experience from one animal to another. When the cat comes home, he cannot tell you what he has seen. And this is not because he has no leisure, for the busy bees can tell each other that they have found honey; it is because he has no symbols. Without symbols history contracts into a plurality of incommunicable autobiographies, and science into each organism's private rules of thumb.

Everybody admits this when it is put to him, but some will urge that this very fact shows the minor importance of words. For it shows that words are means, not ends. They are to be used, not contemplated.

This is also a mistake. Tools cannot be used well without being also contemplated from time to time. Their use must be learnt. In the case of words, learning the use of them is word-thing definition. And the study of word-thing definition corresponds to critical reflection on one's current methods of learning the use of tools, to see whether it can be improved.

The phrase 'merely verbal' is dangerous. What does it mean? A sentence might be called merely verbal on the ground that

(1) it is a noise without a meaning;
(2) it is a tautology;
(3) it is about words;
(4) it cannot give anyone new knowledge.

Then is word-thing definition merely verbal in any of these ways? If we want to answer summarily, the truest answer would be that word-thing definition is not merely verbal in any sense.

1. It is certainly not verbal in the sense of being a noise without meaning. The word-thing definition that 'The Greek word "ὕλη" means wood' is just as significant, and significant in much the same way, as the statement that the Greeks used an upward jerk of the head to symbolize negation. Both are condensed reports of a huge number of historical events.

2. Is word-thing definition 'merely verbal' in the sense

of being a tautology? A tautology is a true proposition whose truth follows from its meaning alone. In order to discover whether a proposition is true, we usually have first to find out what it means and secondly to compare its meaning with the facts. But there are certain peculiar propositions in which the second operation is unnecessary because the truth-value of the proposition is settled by its meaning alone. Such are 'Oxford is Oxford' and 'Oxford is not Oxford'. A proposition that is false by its meaning alone is a contradiction, and a proposition that is true by its meaning alone is a tautology.

Lexical word-thing definitions are not tautologies, for their truthvalue does not depend on their meaning alone, but also on the facts of human behaviour. Whether it is true that 'The old English word "buss" meant kiss' depends on how the English used to talk. Stipulative word-thing definitions are not tautologies, for they are not statements at all.

(This fact, that word-thing definitions are never tautologies, is liable to be denied because word-thing definitions of certain kinds immediately give rise to tautologies. But a word-thing definition is distinct from the tautology which it immediately generates. For example, the nominal definition that 'The word "buss" means kiss' is distinct from the tautology that 'A buss is a kiss'. I develop this point in Chapter VI, § 5.)

3. Is word-thing definition 'merely verbal' in the sense of being about words? Yes, it is; but there are two very big facts to be kept in mind here. The first is that words are immensely important to us, and therefore the fact that a sentence is about words does not involve that the sentence is unimportant to us. In the phrase 'merely verbal' the word 'merely' tends to suggest unimportance; but in so far as it does that the doctrine that word-thing definition is merely verbal is not true but grossly false. And the other fact which we must keep in mind here is that words are essentially means by which *humans* deal with *things*, so that a sentence about words is necessarily also a sentence about humans and things. It would be absurd to infer, from a sentence's being about words, that it was not at all about people or things.

The attempt to write a sentence that is about words without being also about people and things is doomed to failure, and will probably end in a sentence about noises in the air or marks on paper; for marks and noises become words only when they are used by a *person* to signify an *object*. The statement that ' "ύλη" means wood' is as much about words as any statement can be, but it is also about the ancient Greeks and about wood.

4. Is word-thing definition merely verbal in the fourth sense, that it cannot give anyone new knowledge? Emphatically, no. On the contrary, word-thing definitions always give new knowledge to those to whom they are new.

Let us develop this point by distinguishing between (1) the word, which is a symbol, and (2) the thing, symbolized by the word, and (3) the rule that this word symbolizes this thing.

1. A word or symbol is a recognizable sensible form deliberately produced as a sign. The form is usually audible, as spoken words, or visible, as written words or signal flags, because the distance senses are far the most widely useful; but it could be sensible in any way, and tangible forms are regularly used by the blind.

It is sometimes important to distinguish between the general form of the word, repeatable as desired at any time and place, and each particular manifestation of this general form, for example, between the general audible form of the word 'duty', and its particular occurrences, two of which were Nelson's use of it at Trafalgar and Churchill's use of it in 1940. For our purpose, however, it will usually be unnecessary to consider whether we are referring to a form or to a particular occurrence of that form.

2. The word 'thing' is here used in a very broad sense to cover anything, whether a separate enduring physical object like a ball, or a momentary event like an explosion, or a character like sphericality, or a doctrine like liberalism, or anything else at all that can possibly be symbolized by a single word. A word can be a 'thing', because it can be symbolized by another word; but its function as a word can always be distinguished from its status as a 'thing'. The 'thing' meant need not be particular, nor material, nor

independent, nor long enduring. It need never exist at all, as the thing meant by the word 'phlogiston' never exists at any time or place. It need not even be logically possible. The thing meant by the word 'infinitesimal' is selfcontradictory. None of this prevents the thing from being the meaning of some word: Our term 'thing', therefore, means anything whatever, occurrent or nonoccurrent, selfconsistent or selfcontradictory, so far as it is the meaning of some word.

If at any time I need a more specialized word than 'thing' for that which is meant by some word, I shall use 'object' or 'significate' or Charles Morris's 'significatum'. There is no occasion to use Ogden and Richards's word 'referent', which has two great disadvantages. By using an active participle to express the passive idea of being referred to, it has an unpleasant aesthetic effect. And it is explicitly connected by its creators with the false doctrine that all referents are occurrences, so that, if anybody seems to mean by some word something that never occurs, this must be explained away. This is the causal theory of meaning, that the referent of a sign is always some event that actually occurred and helped to cause the sign.

3. If this word means this thing to any persons at any time, these persons have a rule, or a custom, or a habit, by which they habitually take that word as a sign of that thing; and this habit or custom or rule is what is here called: (3) the rule that this word symbolizes this thing.

A lexical word-thing definition is an assertion that there was among certain people a rule or custom or habit by which a certain form was used as a sign of a certain thing. A legislative word-thing definition is a proposal or request in a certain book that there shall be such a rule. Therefore anyone who for the first time hears and understands and believes a particular word-thing definition gets new knowledge or belief to at least this extent, that he learns that there was, or is proposed to be, a rule or custom that this word is a sign of this thing. If he does not learn at least that there is a rule linking just this word to just this object, the definition is not successful. He need not learn any more than this, for he may be already familiar with the word as a sensible form, and with the fact that this form is used as a sign, and with the thing it is used to signify. Thus a man may be familiar with the written form 'Tag', and know that the Germans use this form as a sign of something, and also be familiar with the day, before he learns that the Germans use 'Tag' to mean the day. Anyone who already knows the rule has no need of the definition, for the definition is precisely the report or establishment of the rule; and anyone who is coming to know the definition for the first time is coming to know at least the rule for the first time.

Now that is very important knowledge. It is the acquirement of vocabulary, which is the largest part of learning language. It gives the power to interpret the past and, if the word belongs to a living language, to influence the future. It is part of the acquirement of the most distinctively human power. To belittle it seems a great mistake. To suggest that it is of no philosophical interest is a case of the error we have already described, dividing study into departments and preventing communication between them.

But this is not all the knowledge that a word-thing definition may give. Suppose a man who has never heard the German word 'Tag', and who asks what is the German for day and is told. This man like the former one learns the existence of a certain rule among the Germans. Unlike the former one he also learns the existence of the word 'Tag'. He learns both the rule and the word. A man who meets the word 'parallelepiped' for the first time in a sentence defining its meaning also learns both the rule and the word. Such an event is very common.

This second piece of new knowledge, which the second man obtains in addition to what the first obtains, is nowhere near so important as the first piece. Whereas the knowledge that the rule exists is a powerful instrument for many sorts of understanding and action, the knowledge that the word exists is useful only in linguistics. Nevertheless, it is also knowledge, with many manifestations and much human interest.

There is yet a third sort of knowledge that may be conveyed by word-thing definition, and that is the knowledge of the thing. Whereas a man who learns the definition of

'Tag' is already familiar with the day, and therefore gains no new knowledge of things from this definition, a man who learns the definition of 'derivative' in mathematics nearly always learns thereby for the first time the nature and possibility of the thing. In coming to know for the first time the rule that this word is the name of this thing, he is also coming for the first time to know of the existence or possibility of this thing. The definition gives him a new idea. In this way word-thing definitions, whose purpose is to teach the meanings of words, inevitably also teach the contents of the world and the variety of human ideas. A person who asks what 'compound fracture' means may realize for the first time the possibility of what it means in being given the answer. The greater part of the medical student's knowledge of anatomy comes to him in the form of definitions. Learning new words in one's own language is usually also learning new things. Arthur Pope's definition of the word 'saturation' as applied to colours is unintelligible to me. This is because I cannot distinguish the *thing* to which he means the word to refer. If I came to understand his definition, I should be learning not merely how Pope uses a word, but also a new aspect of visual tones which I have not yet discriminated. Even when we are somewhat familiar with the thing before we learn the definition, the definition may give us new knowledge of the thing in that it abstracts it and sets it off from the rest of the world in a way which we probably had not done before unless we already had some other word for that thing.

Thus it is finally obvious that word-thing definition may convey knowledge not merely about words but also about things, and that the knowledge it conveys about things may be of any kind, including the most important kind.

It does not follow, and it is not true, that 'all words should be defined before they are used'; and a blanket command to 'define your terms' would do far more harm than good if anyone tried to obey it. On the contrary, we should try to arrange our discourses so that we do not have to interrupt ourselves in order to define how we are using our terms. Furthermore, it is not true that we should always use a word in the same sense. To do so would often hamper and complicate discourse very much, while using a word in more than one sense often leads to no error. For example, there are vast areas of study in which no error arises from our using the word 'knowledge' now to mean a mental state and now to mean a body of facts known.

On the other hand, this rejection of the sweeping assertion that 'every term should be defined before it is used' is taken by some persons as justifying them in refusing to give a definition when it is asked for. But from the falsity of 'all words should be defined before they are used' it does not follow that we are under no obligation to define one of our terms when our readers ask us to do so. It is irrational for an author to refuse to try to say what he meant by a certain word in a certain place, and irrational for his interpreter to refuse to do this for him. He may properly say that he no longer knows what he meant by the word. He may also properly say that, although he believes he means something by the word, he is unable at present to find any other words to mean the same thing, that is, he is unable to think of any method of defining his word. But he may not simply declare that he is under no obligation to define the word; for that would be equivalent to saying that he has a right to publish unintelligibilities. It would be interesting to examine whether Santayana has observed these proprieties with regard to his favourite word 'spirit', and whether they are implicitly denied in the following passages.

'Those who insist that every term must be defined clearly before it is used will find no satisfaction in Kant. On the other hand I see no reason to hold that a simple view, sharply defined, is for that reason likely to be correct; and I believe it is more important to discover, if we can, what Kant is talking about than it is to seek perfect precision in the definition of words.'[1]

'It is wrong to tie down the advocates of the coherence theory to a precise definition. What they are doing is to describe an ideal that has never yet been completely clarified but is none the less immanent in all our thinking.'[2]

[1] H. J. Paton, *Kant's Metaphysic of Experience*, I 407. Is there here an implication that what Kant is talking about can be discovered independently of what the definition is of the words he uses?
[2] A. C. Ewing, *Idealism*, p. 231.

III
LEXICAL DEFINITION

§ 1. The Nature of Lexical Definition. Lexical definition is that sort of word-thing definition in which we are explaining the actual way in which some actual word has been used by some actual persons.

It is obvious that lexical definition is something that really happens. Parents, teachers of foreign languages, and probably all persons at some time or other, engage deliberately in the business of telling a person the meaning of a sign. Whatever supposed sorts of definition may turn out to be mare's nests, this sort is real. The child asks what 'magenta' means and the parent tells him. The pupil asks what 'soif' means and the teacher tells him.

Lexical definition is a form of history. It refers to the real past. It tells what certain persons meant by a certain word at a certain less or more specified time and place. In a 'modern' dictionary the time meant is the most recent period down to the instant of writing, and there is a strong expectation that the same persons will continue to use this word in the same way for a considerable future time after the publication of the dictionary. This expectation will very probably be verified for most of the words and falsified for a few. The dictionary is much less reliable as prediction than as history. The future of languages never perfectly resembles their past.

There are altogether three persons involved in lexical definition, first the definer who is explaining the meaning of the word, second the hearer to whom the meaning is being explained, and third the people whose usage of the word gives it whatever meaning it has. Thus Dr. Johnson (person 1) in his dictionary attempted to tell his readers (person 2) what Englishmen of the eighteenth century (person 3) meant by the word 'pastern'. Always this third person must be there, if the sign is to be a sign and the lexical definition of it a reasonable enterprise. The question 'What does this word mean?' is more accurately: 'What do (or did) certain persons use this word to mean?' All meaning is meaning by or for some living thing. The meaning of a word is what it means to some person or persons. It may mean nothing to anybody now, like a lost language; but it must have meant something to somebody once, or it is not and never was a sign. To talk of a sign that means nothing to anybody is either to contradict oneself or to say that the thing is not really a sign. The relation to a person who uses it or understands it is essential to the occurrence of a sign. The less clear the definer makes it who precisely is the third person he is talking about, the less useful his definition. We want to know whether this is what the word meant to the majority of Englishmen or only to a few, and whether in other centuries also or only in this one, and so on.

This essential third person is, however, unconsciously ignored by most of the people who use dictionaries. They look upon a dictionary not as they look upon a book of history but rather as they look upon a book of mathematical tables. A table of square roots is not history. It is a table of eternal facts that were not made by men and cannot be unmade by them, but must be followed and respected if men are to succeed in their purposes. When we wish to infer the diameter of a circular floor from its area, we must either obey the table of square roots or get a false answer. As the square root of 1,369 is and always must be 37, no matter what any human may have thought or said or done, and this fact is pretty sure to be accurately stated in one's book of mathematical tables, so, men think, the meaning of a word is and always must be such and such, no matter how men have actually spoken and written, and this eternal and independent meaning is pretty sure to be accurately stated in one's dictionary. As the engineer who goes against the mathematical tables comes to grief, they think, the writer or speaker who goes against the dictionary comes to grief. They do not, however, clearly represent to themselves what sort of grief he comes to. In particular, they do not think that he becomes unintelligible, but rather that he becomes improper, or vulgar, or uneducated, or in some other way liable to contempt.

Such are the ideas of the majority about dictionaries, and they have probably been shared by the majority of the dictionary-writers themselves.

Yet it is perfectly clear, when we reflect on the matter, that the meanings of words cannot possibly be independent of man as square roots are. A word is a man-made contrivance, and its meaning can only be what some man means by it. The third person must be there.

From which it seems to follow that a good dictionary would be only history. Why is it then that most of the users and most of the makers of dictionaries regard them not as histories but as authorities like a table of square roots?

It is because we have strong and ineradicable feelings of approval and disapproval about the various ways of using words. There are men who cannot help feeling a stab of contempt for one whom they hear splitting an infinitive, or pronouncing 'garage' to rhyme with 'carriage', or using 'transpired' to mean 'occurred'. At every time in every language there are variations in usage or dialect that make no difference to intelligibility. Some of these variations are seized upon as indicators and carriers of differences in human excellence. If one class of the community is more admired or envied or respected than another, and this class has some peculiarities of dialect, those peculiarities become indicators and carriers of excellence. At least, this always happens in communities where there is a formal education in the study of written documents. Then the desire to be excellent and to be considered excellent will always be at work pushing people to discover and adopt the dialect of the preferred class. To assist them in this, books will be written recording the dialect of the preferred class. Among such books are most dictionaries.

Dictionaries, then, tend to be histories not of all the usages prevailing at a given time and place but of those of the preferred group of persons. The average small one-language dictionary is designed largely to enable people to talk and write without arousing contempt in the preferred class. Certain undesirable usages are recorded but characterized as '(vulg.)'. Desirable usages are given no special description, for it is understood that the general purpose of the book is precisely to give the desirable meanings.

The bigger and more scientific the dictionary, the more this purpose of teaching socially correct vocabulary yields to the purpose of recording actual vocabulary. But even the huge *Oxford English Dictionary* teaches as well as records. For example, it urges us to write '-ize' and not '-ise' in all cases descended from the Greek '-ιζειν'.

Dictionaries, therefore, usually do not give us very pure cases of lexical definition. At the best, they mostly tend only to give us true lexical definitions of the vocabulary of a respected class. At the worst they go beyond this to some ideal dialect invented by grammarians. Their aim is to get us accepted by the educated rather than to describe how men have actually spoken and written.

The authoritative character, therefore, which we feel to belong to the dictionary as much as to the table of square roots is the authority of the laws not of number or of inanimate nature, but of human nature driving us to seek excellence and the reputation of excellence, and of human customs and taboos placing goodness and badness now in one set of usages and later in another.

A large dictionary commonly makes various other kinds of assertion about a word besides the fundamental lexical one that certain persons use the word to mean a certain thing; and one of these other kinds had better be noticed here. If the lexicographer disbelieves in the existence of the thing meant by the word, he often expresses his disbelief. Thus he will define 'phlogiston' as 'the supposed cause of fire'. Those who used the word 'phlogiston', however, did not mean by it the supposed cause of fire; they meant the real cause of fire. If we take the word 'supposed' as part of the meaning of 'phlogiston' it makes the definition false. It is really the lexicographer's way of adding his opinion that there is no such thing. He does this because all of us, as soon as we learn the meaning of a word, always wish to have an opinion whether such a thing really occurs. When he omits the word 'supposed', when he defines 'soul' simply as 'the immortal part of man', he by contrast implies that he believes there is such a thing.

§ 2. **Settlement of Two Disputes concerning Lexical Definition.** The answers to some of the disputed questions about definition are now obvious as far as concerns lexical definition.

1. Has a definition a truthvalue? It is obvious that a lexical definition has a truthvalue. Dr. Johnson's definition of 'pastern' was false, and false in just the same sense as if he had said that King George was a woman. The people, whose language the dictionary was supposed to be about, did not use the word in the way he said they did. Lexical definitions are historical assertions, and all historical assertions are true or false in so far as they are definite.

Those who wish to minimize the part played by truth and falsity in definition may here make the following remark: 'The lexical definition that "Hund" means dog is a way of saying that the Germans follow the rule of uttering the word "Hund" when they wish to signify a dog, and of thinking of a dog when they hear the word "Hund". It is a way of saying that the Germans observe a certain rule of meaning. Now a rule has no truthvalue; it cannot be either true or false. And the important thing here is the rule.'

This remark, however, is consistent with lexical definition's having a truthvalue. Though a rule is neither true nor false, a statement that certain people observe a certain rule is either true or false, and a lexical definition is such a statement. As to the opinion that 'the important thing here is the rule', if this is only a report of the objector's interests and preferences, it must be accepted, and it does not contradict anything we have said. If it means that the rule is *an* important matter, it is true and again innocuous. If it means that the rule is more important than the statement that the rule exists, it is hardly decidable, for the two things are important in such different contexts. If lastly it means that the statement that the rule exists is unimportant, it is false.

2. Should lexical definition come at the end, or at the beginning?

The doctrine that definition should come at the end (or at the beginning) appears to be intended as a piece of advice, either for scientific method or for literary composition. It seems to mean either that, if you wish to discover truths, you had better concern yourself with definitions last (or first), or that, if you wish to write clear and convincing expositions, you had better put your definitions at the end (or beginning) of them.

In any case this proposed rule is suspiciously sweeping. It seems very unlikely that there would be one and only one right place for definitions in all scientific investigations or in all writings.

The rule is also suspiciously vague. Definitions of what, we naturally ask, should come at the end of what? Does it mean, for example, that all the definitions given in a book should be given at the end of that book and only at the end?

The idea most commonly in the mind of those who say that definition should come at the end is that, if a book is an inquiry into the nature of beauty, there should be a definition of beauty at the end of that book and none elsewhere in the book. In general, if a book is about a subject S, S should be defined at the end of the book and only there.

Those who hold the view that definition should come at the end have real definition much more in mind than lexical definition. They are thinking, for example, of an effort to analyse and understand better the thing beauty, not of the enterprise of teaching a Russian how to use the English word 'beauty'. They assume that the readers of the book already know the meaning of the word 'beauty' in the ordinary sense of 'know the meaning of', and want to go on to an unusually thorough study of the thing meant by this word.

When Socrates in the *Phaedrus* declared that there should be a definition of the subject at the beginning of a speech, he, too, was thinking of real definition. He was not regarding 'Eros' as an unknown word that had to be explained to the listeners. He was assuming that the word 'Eros' would serve without any explanation to direct their attention to a certain thing, and that the clever speaker would then make them regard this thing in a certain light by giving a real definition of it.

Has the doctrine that definition should come at the end (or at the beginning) any application to our present subject, lexical definition? While there are no absolute rules for literary composition, it seems probable that, at least in the overwhelming majority of informative as opposed to poetic writings, it is a bad thing to leave one's reader long in doubt or in error about the meanings of one's words. It follows that, if the composition contains any words liable to be

misunderstood or not understood at all by the reader, those
words should be lexically defined where they occur, whether
at the end or the beginning or the middle. The place to
define the word is where you first use it, wherever that may
be, though a list of all such definitions in one part of the work
is also valuable.

A special case is when the purpose of the composition is
precisely to discover the lexical definition of some word,
as in Professor Kemp Malone's article 'On Defining
"Mahogany" '.[1] Here the definition is to be reached and
recommended by collecting and criticizing evidence. At
what points in the discussion should the definition be stated?
The definition here is a scientific hypothesis, as to what actual
carpenters and traders have actually meant by 'mahogany' in
the last three centuries; and the question here appears to be
an ordinary case of the question how the evidence for a
scientific hypothesis should be marshalled in an essay and at
what point the hypothesis should be introduced. It is most
unlikely that there is only one good answer. The two following methods have often been very successfully used; that
where the hypothesis is gradually led up to by the evidence,
but not stated until the reader is well prepared to think it
true; and that where the hypothesis is stated both before and
after the evidence.

The doctrine, then, that definition should come at the end
(or at the beginning) has no value as far as concerns lexical
definition. The best maxim that we have discovered regarding the position of lexical definition in literary compositions
is the obvious one that obscure or misunderstandable words
should be defined where they are introduced.

§ 3. **Nothing is lexically indefinable.** Is everything
lexically definable, or are some things lexically indefinable?

When we have to answer briefly, the best answer is that
everything is lexically definable and nothing is lexically
indefinable. But a better insight can be obtained by a series
of qualifications.

In the first place, lexical definition applies only to signs.
It makes no more sense to talk of lexically defining something
that is not a sign than to talk of proceeding eastwards from

[1] *Language*, XVI 308.

the north pole. So it is better to say: all signs are lexically definable and no sign is lexically indefinable.

In the second place, do we mean that every sign is lexically definable by everybody to everybody at every time and place, or that every sign is lexically definable by somebody to somebody at some time and place? Evidently the latter. It is impossible to define the mathematical sense of 'limit' to an average person five years old. A people without writing may have to try for several weeks before they can teach the meanings of some of their words to a visiting anthropologist. There are infinitely many occasions on which some particular enterprise of lexical definition is impossible owing to unfavourable circumstances. We mean only to assert that there is no sign that must by its nature be always lexically indefinable in all circumstances. Every sign is lexically definable to some not impossible human being in some not impossible circumstances.

Thirdly, signs may be used either for communication or for private inference. Probably most people sometimes feel in their own bodies sensations which are to them signs that they are going to feel another sensation. They cannot use these signifying sensations for communicating with anyone else, because they cannot produce these sensations at will, either in others or in themselves. Such signs are lexically indefinable and useful only for private inference.

Our doctrine is that every communicable sign is lexically definable. For no sign can be used in communication unless its meaning can be made known to the person with whom you wish to communicate. If therefore any sign is lexically indefinable to Mr. A, that sign is useless for communicating with Mr. A; and if any sign is lexically indefinable to everybody, that sign is useless for all communication. In other words, all signs successfully used in communication are lexically definable.

Logicians have brought several arguments against this doctrine. J. S. Mill held that proper names are indefinable because they are meaningless.[1] But it is a complete mistake that proper names are meaningless. A meaningless sign is a sign that fails to be a sign, for the essence of a sign is to

[1] *A System of Logic*, I viii, § 1.

mean. A meaningless sign is like a dead man or a blind eye. But proper names are not all failures or mutilations or deaths. Most of them are perfectly successful in meaning the object they are supposed to mean. Hence this argument for indefinability fails entirely.

A much commoner argument for indefinability has been that definition proceeds by analysis and many things are unanalysable. Locke wrote that 'the names of simple ideas, and those only, are incapable of being defined. The reason whereof is this, that the several terms of a definition signifying several ideas, they can all together by no means represent an idea which has no composition at all.'[1]

Of the two premisses of this argument, the one which says that there are unanalysable things is often denied or doubted. That we cannot see how to analyse an object does not prove that it is unanalysable, and it is sometimes suggested that we have not yet, in the course of our analysis, reached any unanalysable object and have no good reason for believing that analysis cannot go on for ever. In any case, the redness that seemed unanalysable to Locke is analysed into chroma, saturation, and value.

The other premiss is still more probably false. That the definition of a name can only proceed by the analysis of a thing is a doctrine that seems likely only to people who are still confusing nominal with real definition. Real definition is a process of analysing things; but word-thing nominal definition is a process of indicating or establishing the meaning of a symbol, and this can be done in several other ways besides giving an analysis of the thing meant, as will be developed in the chapter on methods.

Therefore this argument for indefinability is also a failure, as far as concerns lexical definition.

A third argument that has been given for lexical indefinability is that to define a word we use other words, and if we then wish to define those words we must use still other words, and this cannot go on for ever, so that in our last definition we shall necessarily be using undefined words. There is, of course, also the possibility that our last definition should use only words defined in earlier definitions, so that

[1] *Essay*, iii iv. 6.

the whole chain would return upon itself and form a ring; but such circularity is felt to rob all the definitions of all their value. Hence it is concluded that, to get words defined in a satisfactory way, we must be content to leave some other words indefinable.

The plausibility of this argument is due to a confusion of ideas. Are we trying to teach a man the meaning of words, or to construct a logical system? In constructing logical systems, people usually wish that as many as possible of the simple symbols in the system shall have their meaning uniquely determined by the propositions in the system, and they express this by saying that they want to minimize the number of 'undefined terms' in the system. In this enterprise we cannot avoid either having some 'undefined terms' or making the system a circular set of definitions. If this is what is unambiguously meant by the statement that 'there must be indefinable words', it is true; but it has nothing to do with lexical definition. Lexical definition is our name for the enterprise of teaching some man the meaning actually borne by some word in some society; and there are no lexically indefinable words for the simple reason that it is possible to teach a man every word in the language. To say that there are some lexically indefinable words in the Basque language of 1940 would be to say that the Basques in 1940 used some words whose meaning can never possibly be discovered or taught, which is clearly not so, in principle at any rate. We are bound to make mistakes if we fail to distinguish the ideals and possibilities of logical systems from the enterprise of telling a person what some other persons mean by a word. The latter is theoretically possible for every genuine word (as opposed to meaningless noises pretending to be words), a fact which is correctly expressed in our terms by saying that no word is lexically indefinable.

In a work of logic or mathematics the terms called undefined are often defined in our sense; that is, the author means something by them and he uses expressions from which a suitable reader can discover what he means by them. But he calls them undefined terms because the expressions which explain their meaning do not consist wholly of terms belonging to his system, but are drawn at least in part from the

general stock of common language.[1] If a logical or mathematical system is to be interpreted, that is, applied to some
reality other than itself, every term in it must be defined.
This will be done by giving each of the 'undefined terms'
what is sometimes called an 'interpretative' definition in this
connexion, that is, simply a nominal definition in the present
sense, a statement connecting the term to something else as
that which the term is to mean. Dr. Sigmund Koch called it
'coordinating definition' in the *Psychological Review* for
1941, because it correlates empirical constructions to the
formal terms of the postulate-set, and thus transforms an
abstract system into an empirical one.

Some words would be lexically indefinable, however, if it
were true as the above argument premises that 'to define
a word we always use other words'. All words would be
lexically indefinable if that were true, and so no words would
be understood and language would not exist. Every individual's first words must be taught him by a process that
uses no other words; and they are. Lexical definition therefore sometimes achieves its purpose by a method that uses
no word except the one being defined. This point is
developed in the chapter on method.

Thus this argument, too, fails to establish the occurrence
of indefinable words.

Fourthly, the following rare type of argument for the
existence of indefinable words is occasionally found. It is
occasionally suggested that certain of the symbols used by
men in communicating with each other never need lexical
definition because the understanding of them is innate. Some
such doctrine appears fairly clearly in Pascal's essay on *The
Spirit of Geometry*, and exemplifies the confusion between the
enterprise of teaching men words and the enterprise of
setting up a logical system (in this case a geometrical system).
Pascal points out that the geometrician defines most of his
terms but not all. There are a few undefined terms with
reference to which all the rest are defined. These words are
indefinables, humanly speaking. This at first seems to be a
defect, which must make all our expressions confused; but

[1] For example, Tarski, *Introduction to Logic*, enlarged and revised ed., New
York, pp. 117–18, 120–1.

Pascal declares that nature has avoided that by somehow bringing it about that 'this expression, time, makes everyone think of the same object'. Some words, he holds, indicate their significates so *naturally* that any attempt to illuminate them would produce more darkness than instruction. Indefinability is therefore a perfection rather than a defect. It arises from extreme evidence.

Samuel Johnson also tended to believe that there are 'words too plain to admit a definition'; and a similar notion of indefinability occurs in W. E. Johnson (I 105–6).

What is the truth about this argument? Are there any words whose meanings are known to us by nature, without human art? The phrase 'by nature' becomes very puzzling and misleading when applied to man instead of being opposed to him; but at any rate it is clear that no one ever knows 'by nature' the meaning of any word that is not actually spoken around him. Perhaps, however, there are nonverbal symbols, such as gestures and facial expressions, whose meaning is known to us innately and does not have to be learned and taught. For our present purpose we do not have to decide this point. Instead, we can observe that, even if it is so, it does not establish the conclusion that there are indefinable words, but only that there are words that do not need to be defined. If there are symbols whose meaning is innately known to us, they never *require* lexical definition; but, on the other hand, they would always *admit* it, as every conceivable word that is useful in communication must admit lexical definition. Thus Pascal and W. E. Johnson are using 'indefinable' in the fanciful sense of never requiring definition, not in the ordinary sense of never admitting it.

Thus this argument also fails to establish lexical indefinability. (Nevertheless, Pascal's essay on *The Spirit of Geometry* is about the clearest and truest thing ever written on definition.)

In addition to these four arguments for the occurrence of lexical indefinability, we may notice three causes of this belief which cannot be used as arguments for it. One of these is the emotional power attaching to certain words, as to 'good', 'religion', 'democracy', 'art'. This emotion works to make people think those words indefinable in the following way. They do not distinguish between the emotional and the indicative power of a word, but regard its whole power as being indicative. They then try to define what it indicates. All their attempts seem to themselves to be unsuccessful, the reason of which, though they do not say this to themselves, is that their defining phrases, however accurately they reproduce the indicative power of the definiendum, do not also reproduce its emotion. From this persistent lack of success they infer that the word is indefinable. The unrecognized emotional or volitional force of certain words is thus a cause of their being thought indefinable. But when we recognize it we can describe the emotional power of a word nearly as well as its indicative power, and the word is no longer indefinable. (The method by which we describe the emotional power of a word is discussed in Chapter V, § 9.)

A second cause that often makes us believe a word indefinable is an undetected ambiguity in the word. If a word has two senses, but we, thinking it univocal, try to give one single definition of it, every answer we can think of will fail to cover one of the senses, so that it can be refuted by producing an example to which the word is applied in that sense. And this persistent failure will suggest that the word is indefinable.

There is a third cause of the belief that certain words are indefinable. We have seen that, in learning a lexical definition, a man may be not merely coming to know that this word means this thing but also coming to know the existence or possibility of this thing for the first time. Thus in learning the definition of 'dodecahedron' he probably thinks for the first time in his life of the possibility of constructing a solid out of sides that are regular pentagons; and in learning that 'automobile' means a car that moves by itself he might think for the first time of a car that moved by itself. In these cases a definition proceeding entirely by words, without any pointing of the finger or other physical introduction, succeeds in giving the learner not merely the new knowledge that a certain word is the name of a certain thing but also the new idea that such a thing is possible.

There are other cases, however, in which this is impossible. There are words whose definition never gives the learner his first idea of that thing by verbal means alone. There are words whose meaning cannot be made known to a person unless either he has actually experienced the thing meant or he is made to experience it in the process of definition itself, which therefore is not merely verbal but includes pointing or something like it. Such, for example, is the word 'moves' in the above definition of 'automobile'. Although a wholly verbal definition of an 'automobile' could give the idea of an automobile to a man who had never seen or thought of one, no definition of the word 'moves' could give the idea of movement to a man unless he either had already experienced movement or were made to experience it in the course of the definition itself. And the names for all the simple, ultimate qualities of our experience are of this nature. They are names that can be made significant only to persons who have actually experienced the quality meant or are given actual experience of it in the defining process itself.

The words, of which a merely verbal definition can teach us not merely the rule that this word means this thing but also the possibility of this thing, are, we believe, the words that mean things that are complexes of things we have experienced. Mere words can give us the idea of a new complex, provided it is a complex only of things we have already experienced. Mere words cannot give us the idea of a new thing if we have never experienced it and it is not a complex of things we have experienced.

This difference is the key to many persons' conviction that there are indefinable words. They include in their working definition of 'definition', not merely that a man teaches a second man that a certain word means a certain thing, but also that the thing in question comes as a new idea to the learner, which he has not experienced or thought of before. It follows then that those words whose meaning can be taught only to those who already have experienced the thing are indefinable names. Such, for example, is Locke's train of thought.

But this is an inconvenient and misleading usage. We need a name for the mere process of imparting the rule that this word means this thing, whether or not the idea of this thing is new to the learner of the rule. And the name marked

out for it by the history of language is 'definition'. Any
teaching that a certain word is the name for a certain thing
should be called 'definition', whether or not it is also a first
introduction of the thing. The reluctance to use the word
'definition' in this broad sense is a mere relic of the confusion
of nominal definition with real definition, for real definition
is a process of getting new knowledge of things. That the
broad sense is the right one is strongly indicated by the fact
that Locke, while he uses the word in the narrow sense,
defines it in the broad one. While he declines to call the
teaching of the word 'red' a definition, because it cannot
succeed unless the learner has already experienced redness,
he defines definition as 'being nothing but making another
understand by words what idea the term defined stands for',[1]
a process which can certainly often be performed upon the
word 'red'. His state of mind appears fairly clearly in the
following words:

'When any term stands for an idea a man is acquainted with, but is
ignorant that that term is the sign of it, there another name, of the same
idea which he has been accustomed to, may make him understand its
meaning. But in no case whatsoever is any name of any simple idea
capable of a definition.'[2]

If it were right to deny the name of 'definition' to an
explanation of the word 'moves' because it requires previous
experience in the learner, it would be right to deny the name
of 'definition' to all explanation of all words. For all explanation of the meaning of words requires previous experience in the learner at some stage. While the merely verbal
definition of 'automobile' as a self-moving car can give the
idea of an automobile to a man who has never seen one, it
could not do that unless this man had already had experience
of motion and of the simple qualities involved in 'car'. Thus
the idea that there are indefinable words sometimes arises
out of the mistaken idea that we can get new knowledge
independently of experience.

As a pendant to this discussion of lexical indefinability, I will
add some remarks on the closely related topic of ineffability.
Are some experiences ineffable? And what is ineffability?

---

[1] *Essay*, iii iii. 10.   [2] Ibid., iii iv. 14.

'Ineffable' seems to mean unspeakable; but, whereas a thing may be unspeakable merely because it is too horrible or because there is a taboo against naming it, the ineffable is intended to be that sort of unspeakableness which no human, however emancipated, could possibly overcome because it is inherent in the nature of the thing in its relation to the nature of symbols.

One cannot make a symbol for a thing of whose existence one is unaware. People did not and could not make the symbol 'equator' until they realized that there was such a thing. They, could of course, have said: ' "Equator" is a good noise; I should like to use it to symbolize something; at present I don't know of anything to symbolize by this noise, but as soon as I discover something new that needs a name, I will call it "equator".' But such a process is idle, and it is not making a symbol but only preparing a noise to become a symbol in case there is anything to symbolize. In this trivial sense, then, the unknown is ineffable so long as it remains unknown; and if anything is necessarily for ever unknowable, it is necessarily also for ever ineffable.

But the ineffability that anyone is interested in asserting is the ineffability of something that can be known and is known. Is that possible?

Everybody who has a recognizable or rememberable experience or sort of experience can give it a name if he wishes. If he has a peculiar sensation in his leg he can call that sort of sensation 'allig'. If he has a peculiar religious ecstasy he can call that sort of religious ecstasy 'gride'. It is evidently possible for every man to give a name to every element that he can distinguish in his own experience. Nothing is ineffable in the sense of being unnameable by its experiencer.

But will these names, 'allig' and 'gride', ever enable him to make anybody else know what sort of experience he has been having? Will they make his experiences effable in the sense that he can make another party know just what sort of experience he had?

In what circumstances can any word ever make you know what experience I have had? The answer is that I can use the word 'allig' to make you know what sort of experience I am

having, if there is a way by which I can make you have that
sort of experience and at the same time utter the word 'allig'.
I can make you know what I mean by 'pain', because I can
pinch you and say that what you feel then is what I mean
by 'pain'. But if I use the word 'allig' to mean some very
special sort of pain which I sometimes feel, and if I know
no method by which this special sort of pain can be produced
at will, there is no way of telling you precisely what I mean
by 'allig', and the word 'allig' is not a useful tool for describing my experiences to you. If you can see, I can make you
know what experience I mean by 'red' by confronting you
with something red; but if you cannot see I cannot make
you know it.

Thus all sorts of experience are ineffable (that is, we have
no means of surely communicating the fact that we are
having them) in so far as there is no means of producing
them in others at will; and all sorts of experience are effable
in so far as one man can cause another man to have an
experience of that sort and then apply a name to it.

Symbols are not what they symbolize. To utter a name
is not directly to give a man an experience, except the experience of hearing that noise. The uttered word 'red' is not
red, and the uttered word 'ecstasy' is not ecstatic. For a
man to know what experience I mean, there must have been
established in him an association between that symbol and
that experience, and I can establish such an association only
when I have a way of arousing that kind of experience in
him without the use of the symbol.

Wittgenstein wrote that, 'There is indeed the inexpressible. This *shows* itself; it is the mystical.'[1] In a dissertation
in the library of the University of California at Berkeley
Dr. Maslow concurs in the following words:

'We must, I believe, admit that there are inexpressible aspects in our
experience. To deny the inexpressibility of some aspects of our
experience and thus their inaccessibility to communicable knowledge,
is equivalent to the assertion that all and every experience is expressible
and communicable, which is a case of presumptuous and dogmatic
rationalism.'

But anything that shows itself can be named by him to

[1] *Tractatus*, 6. 522.

whom it shows itself, and in this sense everything is expressible. Expressibility does not, however, entail com-
municability as Dr. Maslow implies. The expressible is
communicable only if you and I both express the same sort of
experience by the same name, and this identity of behaviour
can be secured only when there is a means by which one of us
can produce that sort of behaviour in the other at will.
Sometimes there is such a means and sometimes there is
not. For example, if we can both see, there is a means by
which we can be brought to apply the same name to the
experience of redness; if one of us is blind, there is not. If
there is a sort of experience which is open only to a small
minority of humans, those who enjoy it cannot communicate
it to the majority; and whether they can communicate it to
each other depends on whether they have a way of producing
it in each other or knowing when it is occurring in each other.

§ 4. **Lexical Definition can never be Perfect.** Another
of the disputed points about definitions is whether they
should be brief or not. Should lexical definitions be brief?

Lexical definitions are historical statements. They are
scientific statements in the broad sense in which utterance
is either scientific or poetic. Brevity always has both advantages and disadvantages in scientific discourse. It tends
to give speed and to increase one's grasp, but also to lose detail
and accuracy and richness of insight. The more an activity is
pursued for its own sake, the less desirable, as a rule, is brevity.
The nearer an activity comes to being merely a means, the better it is that it should be brief, for a mere means is an unsatis-
fying activity from which we wish to escape. Most lexical
definitions, whose purpose is to make somebody know the
meaning of some word, are merely means to the ulterior purpose of using that word; the quicker this further purpose
can be achieved the better; therefore the shorter the definition
the better.

On the other hand, every brief lexical definition of a word
in common use is grossly inaccurate or at best grossly partial,
because all words that have been used by many people have
many sorts and nuances and dimensions of meaning. That
is why there is room for colossal dictionaries. Hence a lexical
definition even when regarded as a mere tool must often

contain far more than a dozen words; and when the lover
of language undertakes to state the meaning of a word for
its own sake he may well expand his definition to far more
than a dozen pages. Let us bring these facts home to ourselves by calling to mind for a time the complexities of the
actual meanings of words, and the consequent complexities
of accurate lexicography.

Living language is always in flux. All words in common
speech are liable to change their meanings from time to
time. Many of them change their meanings as we pass from
place to place across the earth, notably the common words
for living kinds, such as 'robin' and 'sycamore'. Many more
of them change their meanings as we pass from class to class
in the same place, especially from the common man to the
learned. Most of all they change their meanings as we pass
from age to age. 'Enthusiasm' no longer means what it
meant in the eighteenth century. Copious examples and
long discussions of this perpetual changing are set out in
many philological works, e.g. Hermann Paul's *Prinzi-
pien der Sprachgeschichte*. Even the scientist, consciously
aiming at fixity of reference, often finds his words changing in his hands, or deliberately changes their meanings
to meet a new situation or avoid a greater inconvenience.
Any volume of the periodical *Science* will show instances of
this in biology. For example, as biologists have come to
learn more of the multiplicity of chemical reactions occurring
in living beings, they have had difficulty in keeping the
word 'respiration' to a definite meaning. The mathematician,
dealing with things that do not change or grow in his hands,
or with ideas that do not have to fit the eddies of time and
space, is the least likely to find his words changing their
meanings; but he, too, finds them doing so. The spread of
education on the whole slows down the rate of change; but
it never obliterates it, and in one way it increases it, namely,
by encouraging research, which brings novelties that upset
old nomenclatures.

The flux of language has obvious inconveniences. We
see the man from one country failing to indicate which
specific grain he means to the man from another. We see
a pair of words that were usefully distinct in meaning coming

to be synonymous, as 'paradox' and 'contradiction'. We see slang making a word so ambiguous that we hesitate to use it in its ancient sense without adding explanations; this has recently happened, for example, to the word 'dumb' in U.S.A. A word, we feel, should be like a pair of forceps which could pass the same specimen from hand to hand without fear of losing it; but in fact it is often a prestidigitator who secretly switches the specimen as he conveys it from one man to the next, and we are deceived as to what the other man is talking about. We see thousands of words taking on new meanings, through dozens of different sorts of cause, without losing their old ones, so that they come to be multivocal. We have seen, though perhaps we never shall again, languages that were one throughout an area dividing into dialects more and more estranged from each other until intercommunication ceases.

Hence men have tried to arrest the flux, especially in those ages before the nineteenth century when the conviction had not prevailed that all things are always changing, and not in a cycle but towards something new and unknown. Now it is believed that the universe is on an irresistible process in the evolution of living individuals, in the degradation of energy towards the heat-death, and in many other aspects, and that thought, conditioned by its social circumstances, can never be quite the same as at any previous time. All this represses most enterprises for the fixing of language; but in the eighteenth century Swift issued a serious proposal for such an undertaking. Samuel Johnson tells us in the introduction to his dictionary that he, too, felt the 'wish that the instrument might be less apt to decay, and that signs might be permanent, like the things they denote'. He started, he says, with Swift's hope of fixing the language, but saw it to be impossible. He never ceased, however, to hope to delay the rate of change; and he definitely regarded himself as not merely an historian of what the English language had done, but also in part a legislator of what it should do.

The flux of word-meanings cannot be stopped because its causes cannot be removed. We are told that in illiterate cultures there is sometimes a very rapid change of vocabulary because words easily acquire unfortunate associations

and become taboo; probably this cause will always continue
to operate to some extent, even in the most literate and
emancipated culture man ever achieves. Changes in things
must effect changes in the meanings of words. 'Car' cannot
mean the same now as it did before steam and petroleum
engines. No man has time to study carefully the past meaning of all the words he uses; the major part of his vocabulary
has been acquired without the aid of the dictionary or any
other intentional teaching, by unconscious inference from
examples of its use; and inevitably his inference is often
slightly wrong. Inevitably a degradation, by which a word
of peculiar meaning comes to be only a synonym for an
existing word, is occasionally given prominence and weight
by a great man's use, as when Dickens called a book *Our
Mutual Friend*. To achieve the urgent end of the moment,
we use whatever words occur to us as most efficient then
and there for that purpose; and it is rare that our sole purpose
is to please some academy by preserving the ancient meanings of words.

Men will never forgo the beauties and delights and conveniences of metaphor; and metaphors will always tend to
decay into literal senses, thus changing or adding to the
meaning of the word. Men will always be finding themselves with a new thing to express and no word for it, and
usually they will meet the problem by applying whichever
old word seems nearest, and thus the old word will acquire
another meaning or a stretched meaning. Very rarely will
they do what A. E. Housman bade them do, invent a new
noise to mean the new thing. For they like to feel that they
are not creating language but using an established and
approved language; the closeness of the old sense of the
word to the new sense helps to make the new sense intelligible, and indeed often conceals from everybody the fact
that a new sense has arisen. Such are a few of the causes that
have ensured and will ensure the mutability of language.
Owing to them the meanings of almost every common word
are different at different times and multiple at all times.

And the flux has many advantages too. Its primary advantage is its primary cause: the ability to meet the urgent
needs of the present moment with the vocabulary one has

in store. But this momentary advantage does not always cost a general drawback. On the contrary, the changeability of vocabulary gives it its power to meet the new circumstances, and to express the new ideas, that are always arising.

No brief lexical definition of a word, then, is likely to embrace the multiplicity of uses the word has had at different times or even at one time. A lexical definition could nearly always be truer by being longer. In practice even the largest dictionaries and the fullest definitions are obliged to make a selection, just as any sort of history is a selection, even a thousand-page history of a single day in the life of a single man. The most momentous and unfortunate kind of selection commonly made is that the lexicographer excludes all spoken language and confines himself to the written form. Within the written language he usually further confines himself to the vocabulary of the writers he to some extent approves; and, as he is usually a literary man, this usually means that there is no record of those writings that are completely outside the literary interest, such as notices in barbershops or factories. Selection being inevitable, it is rational to select for record the vocabularies of the writers we value and of the societies whose approval we need or value. The necessity for selection enforces the lexicographer's tendency to become an arbiter instead of an historian.

Even if by a miracle a lexicographer succeeded in giving a complete list of the meanings of a word, he would still not have given a complete account of the word, for the following reasons.

People use two or more senses of a word at the same time, not merely in puns but also for the most serious science and the most profound poetry. Often they would be unable to separate the meanings which the lexicographer analyses. What to him is ambiguity is to them the livingness of language. The dictionary hides the way in which the different meanings of the word are yet one meaning.

A word has other dimensions besides its indicativeness, and a complete account of it would have to give its nature in these other dimensions too. Besides indicating it expresses. A word for x indicates x and expresses the idea of x. When a man says 'grey', he indicates grey and expresses his idea of grey. Every word carries with it, in each speaker's mind in which it lives, certain associations other than its main association to what it indicates, associations to other things or associated emotions and attitudes. No dictionary can record these associations when they are peculiar to one or a few persons, nor needs to. But often the same association holds for nearly all speakers of the language. Often a word arouses nearly the same emotion or attitude in all its users. Then it is very desirable that this emotional or pragmatic dimension should be recorded as well as the indicative dimension. No dictionaries, however, attempt to do this in any thorough or systematic way. They give the emotional dimensions only for certain special cases. Thus a dictionary may say of the word 'nigger': 'negro (now usually contemptuous)', giving first the indicative and then the emotional force of the word. The *Oxford English Dictionary* defines 'good' as 'the most general adj. of commendation, implying the existence in a high, or at least satisfactory, degree of characteristic qualities which are either admirable in themselves or useful for some purpose'; it thus assigns to the word a very definite emotional dimension and almost no indicative dimension. If there are words that have no indicative dimension, but merely express, they are, of course, the words for which the dictionary is most likely to define the emotional dimension.

In most languages each word has specific ways of combining with other words, and may be used in a sentence only in those ways. This may be called the syntactical dimension of the word. Thus 'heavy', 'heaviness', 'heavily', are three words that have exactly the same indicative force, and nearly the same emotional force, but distinct syntactic forces. This dimension, too, must be specified in any complete account of the word. Many dictionaries specify it systematically for all words. That is easy to do in some languages because along this dimension all the words of the language fall into one and only one of a few well-marked classes that have been determined and can be indicated by a brief symbol.

Besides the syntactical relations of a word to the other words in a sentence, there are the relations of the word to the other elements in the context of its occurrence, such as the speaker, his sex, the hearer, his sex, the time, and the place. There are words whose occurrence or non-occurrence is determined in part neither by what is to be indicated nor by what is to be expressed, nor by the other words in the sentence, but by something else in the context. Thus in the Koasati language *ó.t* and *ó.c* both indicate the same thing, namely, 'he is building a fire', and both, so far as I know, express the same emotion and demand the same syntactical function in the sentence; but the former is to be uttered only by a woman and the latter only by a man.[1] There are also, apparently, languages in which one's speech must vary with the sex of one's hearer, even in sentences whose indicative meaning is nothing to do with the hearer.[2]

This contextual dimension is very obvious in words like 'I', 'you', 'he', 'this', 'to-day', 'here'; for in them it controls the indicative reference. What they indicate varies from occasion to occasion because it is determined by the occasion. To-day' is to mean on each occasion the day on which the word is uttered.

The contextual dimension appears to be absent from most words in Indo-European languages. But where it is present a complete lexical definition of the word would include it.

Thus a complete lexical definition of a word might have to define it along four dimensions at least, the contextual, the syntactic, the expressive, and the indicative; and the indicative definition would nearly always be very complex.

So much by way of calling to mind that lexical definition cannot be at once brief and accurate, and that it is a very difficult matter to do well.

[1] Mary Haas in *Language*, XX 144.
[2] See the same article, pp. 148–9.

STIPULATIVE DEFINITION

§ 1. The Nature of Stipulative Definition. We have examined word-thing definition in general, and also the lexical species of it. Let us now examine its other species, the stipulative.

'Whatsoever Adam called every living creature, that was the name thereof.'

Humpty Dumpty insisted that words were to mean what he chose that they should mean. He did not concern himself with any lexical inquiries, that is, with finding out what some set of people actually had meant by some word. He laid down what the word was to mean when he used it. That was stipulative definition.

The maker of dictionaries sometimes regards himself as a legislator rather than as an historian, as saying how words ought to be used rather than how they are used. So far as he does this, he regards himself as giving stipulative definitions, not lexical ones.

Above all, the mathematicians, ever since Euclid at latest, have been making their own meanings for words. 'By a *denumerable* series', they say, for example, 'we shall mean a series which you can put into one-one correspondence with the positive integers without changing its order.' This is not an historical description of what has been meant by 'denumerable' in the past or is commonly meant by it now. It is an announcement of what is going to be meant by it in the present work, or a request to the reader to take it in that sense.

By 'stipulative' word-thing definition, then, I mean the explicit and selfconscious setting up of the meaning-relation between some word and some object, the act of assigning an object to a name (or a name to an object), not the act of recording an already existing assignment. This is the kind of definition that Whitehead and Russell had in mind when they wrote that 'a definition is a declaration that a certain newly introduced symbol . . . *is to mean*', &c.[1]

---

[1] *Principia Mathematica*, 2nd ed., I, p. 11.

When we stipulate that a certain thing is to be the meaning of a certain word, the word may or may not have previously existed as a name for something else. Before the mathematicians began to use 'denumerable' as the name of a species of series, perhaps the word existed as the name of something else, and perhaps it did not exist at all but was invented for this very purpose. Which of these is the fact makes no difference to the nature of stipulative definition; but, in case the word did previously exist as the name of something else, then, as Pascal points out, that previous meaning is entirely annulled by the new stipulation. A stipulative definition stipulates that, whatever the word may mean in other communications or even in earlier parts of this communication, it is for the rest of this communication to be taken as having *no meaning whatever* except the one now stipulated. Any previous meanings are thereby abolished for the remainder of this communication.

The element of deliberate, arbitrary, selfconscious choice of a name for a certain thing, or of a thing for a certain name, is the essential and constant element in what I am calling 'stipulative definition', the element which I believe it important to realize and distinguish. Whether this individual choice agrees with or differs from the common usage of the word defined, and whether there *is* any common usage of it or not, is irrelevant to the essence of stipulation. A stipulative definition may vary, in this respect, all the way from stipulating an entirely novel noise as the name of an entirely novel thing, to merely confirming and adopting common usage. Often it consists merely in adopting one of the many common meanings of a common word and discarding the rest, that is, in announcing which of the established meanings you are going to use. The essence is that stipulative definition is the adoption of elementary sign-uses, while lexical definition is the reporting of them.

A defining sentence, taken out of context, may or may not indicate clearly what kind of definition it means. The following is obviously stipulative:

1. 'Let us mean by a "pencil" a right cylinder whose cross-section is a regular polygon.'

The following is obviously lexical:

2. 'By "pencil" some geometers have meant a right cylinder whose cross-section is a regular polygon.'

But the following might be either, if considered by itself:

3. 'A pencil is a right cylinder whose cross-section is a regular polygon.'

The third type of formula for expressing a definition is very common; and many persons have a feeling that it is the only correct type, the other two not really expressing definitions at all, but, at nearest, larger thoughts in which a definition is an element. They are therefore inclined to say that the present distinction between lexical and stipulative definition is merely a distinction between the various circumstances that may accompany a definition, and fails to show any differentiation of definition itself. Yet surely no one, after reflection, wishes to regard definition merely as a string of words, but rather as a thought or other human activity or else as the object of that thought. If we take it as a human activity, the activity of thinking or communicating that certain persons used a certain word to mean a certain thing is specifically distinct from the activity of choosing a certain word to mean a certain thing.

This type of nominal definition was called 'stipulation' by James Mackaye in his *The Logic of Language*. In Latin the word *stipulatio* was a legal term meaning a promise given on demand, an engagement, agreement, bargain, or contract. This kind of definition has also been called 'imposition', because it is the act of imposing a name upon an object; and 'original definition', because it originates a usage; and 'institution', for the same reason; and 'legislative definition', because it does not report a fact but rather enacts a law. It might also be called 'propositive', or 'invitatory', or 'imperative'. A large part of it, but not the whole, is covered by the notion of 'redefinition'.[1] A smaller part of it is covered by Professor Dubs's 'scientific definition';[2] for he means by this phrase the type of definition most commonly found in works of science, if we exclude works devoted to the scientific study

---

[1] e.g. Mr. John Wisdom in *Mind*, 1941, p. 410.
[2] *Philosophical Review*, 1943, pp. 566–7.

of languages, in which, of course, there are many lexical definitions. In the course of this book I have called it mainly 'stipulative' but sometimes 'legislative' definition. 'Legislative' has the advantage of being more immediately intelligible; but when a verb is required 'legislate' gives a seriously inaccurate impression.

The following division of stipulation into two species is worth noticing. One may give a name to a thing or one may give a thing to a name. Here is an example of giving a name to a thing: 'Some people, when they see another person enjoying goods which they lack, experience bitterness and hate of the enjoyer; in what follows this type of reaction will be referred to as "envy".' And here is an example of giving a thing to a name: 'Is envy really a bad thing?—It depends what you mean by "envy". If you mean feeling bitterness and hate towards a man because he has some good which you lack, then', &c. Each of these is a species of definition because in each we arrive at a rule by which a certain word means a certain thing. They differ in that in one we start from the thing and connect it to a word, while in the other we start from the word and connect it to a thing. They might be called the thing-word and the word-thing forms of definition. The distinction between the thing-word and the word-thing mode of arriving at a nominal definition applies both to stipulative and to lexical definition.

A lexical definition cannot be at the same time brief and perfect, because words in common usage have many meanings. But a stipulative definition is not under this limitation, because it is not an attempt to report the infinite varieties of actual usage but rather an attempt to replace them by a single unambiguous usage. We rarely have a good reason for stipulating that a word is to have more than one meaning.

§ 2. The Truthvalue of Stipulative Definitions. The distinction between lexical and stipulative definition explains the disagreement over the question whether definitions have a truthvalue. Lexical definitions have a truthvalue but stipulative definitions have not. A lexical definition is an assertion that certain people use a certain word in a certain way, and is therefore either true or false. A stipulative definition, however, is not an assertion at all. Therefore, since assertions are the only sentences that have a truth-value, it has no truthvalue. It is more like a *request* to the reader that he will understand the word in a certain way, or a *command*; and these, though significant utterances, have no truthvalue. It is a proposal rather than a proposition. It looks to the future not the past. This is the fundamental reason why it can be brief and yet satisfactory. It does not have, as every true statement has, the task of following the sinuosities of reality. It is an arbitrary choice. If it succeeds in establishing a usage, the subsequent lexical definition of that usage will not be an arbitrary choice. As W. E. Johnson wrote, there is an absolutely first introduction and naming, as at christening a child, and there is an introduction and naming that is relative to a particular person, as in social introductions. The former is arbitrary in a way in which the others are not (I 94–5).

The arbitrariness and the lack of truthvalue that are proper to stipulative definition are often asserted of definition as such. Thus Galileo said that all definitions are arbitrary.[1]

Those who generalize the truth that stipulative definition is neither true nor false into the falsehood that definition as such is neither true nor false are often led into contradiction thereby. Thus James Mackaye in *The Logic of Language* maintains that definition is neither true nor false, but speaks of Plato's dialogue *Euthyphro* as 'verifying' a proposed definition.

But though stipulation *as such* cannot be true or false, it usually *implies* an element of assertion, and consequently of truth or falsehood, in the following way. Every word-thing definition professes to connect a word with a thing, and therefore assumes that the word and the thing both exist in some way. The assumption that the word exists cannot be false in stipulative definition; for in uttering the definition we utter the word and thus make it exist. But it can be false in lexical definition, for the existence there implied is utterance by other persons. The assumption that the thing exists can be false in both kinds of word-thing definition. Thus the geometers who defined 'horned angles' as those made by the intersection of curves as opposed to straight lines were

---

[1] *Two New Sciences*, tr. Crew and De Salvio, New York, 1914, p. 162.

implying and believing in the possibility of such a thing, whereas the angle between any two curves can only be the angle between the two straight lines that are tangent to the curves at the point of intersection. John Stuart Mill remarked that a definition is usually accompanied by a tacit existence-proposition, because he wished to separate the two and maintain that the pure definition has no truthvalue. He did not remark that it is practically impossible to make or receive a word-thing definition without having an opinion about the existence of the object assigned to the word by the definition, whether occurrent or merely imaginary, whether selfconsistent or selfcontradictory. He did not remark that one very common reason for stipulating a new meaning for a word is the discovery of the existence or non-existence of something. Einstein stipulated a new meaning for the word 'simultaneous' because he realized that the only way of determining which distant events are simultaneous with events here is by using electromagnetic waves and that the speed of such waves is the same whatever the speed of their source.

There is still another way in which truth or falsehood enters into stipulative definition. In stipulating a meaning for a word, a writer demands that his reader shall understand the word in that sense whenever it occurs in that work. The writer thereby lays upon himself the duty of using the word only in that sense, and tacitly promises to do so, and tacitly prophesies that he will do so. But sometimes a writer does not use the word only in the sense he has stipulated. Then his stipulation implied a false promise and a false prediction. When he does use the word only in the sense he stipulated, his stipulation implies a true promise and a true prediction. The Port Royal Logic said: 'The definition of names cannot be contested . . . for we cannot deny that a man has given to a sound the signification which he says he has given to it.'[1] This is a complete mistake. We often find a writer evidently using a word in a sense other than the sense he stipulated earlier in the work; and I shall give one or two examples of this on another occasion. It is not necessarily a case of dishonesty. Or at any rate the dishonesty may be in the words themselves rather than in the writer; for words often

[1] Trans. Baynes, p. 81.

deceive their own utterers about what they mean as they are uttered!

Words, wrote Virginia Woolf in *The Death of the Moth* (p. 131):

'Words . . . are the wildest, freest, most irresponsible, most unteachable of all things. Of course, you can catch them and sort them and place them in alphabetical order in dictionaries. But words do not live in dictionaries; they live in the mind. . . . Thus to lay down any laws for such irreclaimable vagabonds is worse than useless. A few trifling rules of grammar and spelling are all the constraint we can put on them. All we can say about them, as we peer at them over the edge of that deep, dark and only fitfully illuminated cavern in which they live—the mind—all we can say about them is that they seem to like people to think and to feel before they use them, but to think and to feel not about them, but about something different. They are highly sensitive, easily made self-conscious. They do not like to have their purity or their impurity discussed. . . . Nor do they like being lifted out on the point of a pen and examined separately. They hang together, in sentences, in paragraphs, sometimes for whole pages at a time. They hate being useful; they hate making money; they hate being lectured about in public. In short, they hate anything that stamps them with one meaning or confines them to one attitude, for it is their nature to change.'

That stipulative definitions lack truthvalue does not prevent words stipulatively defined from being used to make true or false statements. If you stipulate that 'nacks' is to mean roses and 'braze' is to mean smell sweet, it is false that nacks never braze. That there is nothing necessary about the relation between any elementary sign and its meaning does not prevent there being something necessary about some sentences. One plus one is necessarily two although it is not necessary that we should use the word 'one' to name one. The false belief that the arbitrariness of all nominal definitions involves the arbitrariness of all statements was held by Thomas Hobbes according to Leibniz;[1] but I have not yet found it in Hobbes's work.

Stipulative definitions are arbitrary in a way that lexical definitions are not; but in a loose sense they are both arbitrary. In stipulation we freely make any word mean anything we choose, whereas in lexical definition we try to report truly what actual persons have actually meant by the

---

[1] *Opera Philosophica*, ed. J. E. Erdmann, 1840, p. 80.

word. That is the strict sense in which stipulation is arbitrary and lexical definition is not. But they are both arbitrary, and all word-thing definition is arbitrary, in this loose sense that there is no connexion between a word and the thing it means except that some human beings use that word to mean that thing. There is no connexion between the word 'cock-a-doodle-doo' and the cry of a cock except that some people use the one sound to mean the other sound, and mistakenly think that the two sounds resemble each other.

§ 3. **The Advantages and Disadvantages of Stipulative Definitions.** Why do we stipulate? In other words, what are the ulterior purposes of stipulative definition? When our primary purpose is to establish the rule that a certain word signifies a certain thing, we employ certain means to attain this purpose, but this purpose is itself also a means to some further purpose; for we do not stipulate new definitions for the sake of this activity itself.

1. The most obvious advantage we may hope to gain by stipulation is the removal of an ambiguity and the avoidance of an inconvenience caused by the ambiguity. If we see that our hearer is taking one of our words in a sense other than the sense we intend, we interrupt our discourse to tell him which sense we intend. In discussing lexical definition I have developed the doctrine that in most actual language most words are ambiguous. Such an ambiguity is often undesirable. Then we stipulate. Stipulation is thus a means of ensuring that we are all talking about the same thing when we use the same word. In ordinary life it is not the case that people always mean the same species or even the same genus when they talk about 'sparrows', or 'meadowsweet', or 'conjunctivitis', or 'white gold', or 'mahogany'. Learned and professional societies make stipulative definitions in order that intercourse between their members may not be rendered futile by such ambiguities. Thousands of arguments occur every day which are from a scientific point of view quite futile because the arguers either do not realize that they are using a word in different senses, or, if they realize it, devote themselves to condemning all uses of the word but their own. Such was the argument whether, when a man walks round a tree and a squirrel on the trunk keeps diametrically oppo-

site him, he walks 'round' the squirrel. If 'go round' means
to be first north then east then south then west and then
north again of the squirrel, the man does go round the
squirrel. But if it means to be nearest first to the squirrel's
belly then to his right side then to his back then to his left
side and then to his belly again, he does not. In ordinary
speech the phrase 'go round' means ambiguously both; and
a stipulation is required for the unusual case where the two
do not go together.

This is why textbooks of logic very often introduce and
recommend definition with the phrase 'definition is the cure
for ambiguity'. But the doctrine requires more precise
formulation. For it is not definition in general that can be
used as a cure for ambiguity, but only stipulative definition.
Lexical definitions and real definitions do not cure ambiguities. The purpose of lexical definitions is rather merely to
describe ambiguities. The purpose of real definitions is
nothing to do with ambiguity, but fails unless the words used
in it have already been cleared of ambiguities by previous
stipulations. Some forms of real definition create ambiguities rather than cure them.

2. Stipulation of the above kind involves no new rule of
meaning; it is merely the choice of one established rule and
the rejection of others. The more artificial kind of stipulation, to which the more important kinds of stipulation belong, is that which does not adopt an existing rule but creates
a new one. And there are many good ulterior purposes
which justify creating a new rule. Obviously the appearance
of a new object, such as a new comet, justifies the stipulation
of a new rule, that a certain word is to be the name of this
new object. Furthermore, some objects, though old and
familiar, have no established names, because they are not
referred to often enough to require anything but a descriptive phrase. If a change occurs by which such an object
comes to be frequently referred to, it will be given a name
to save time in mentioning it. The name will be verbally
defined as equivalent to the phrase by which the object was
formerly indicated. 'By "Westerland" I shall mean the land
between the Elbe and the Somme.' In both cases the stipulation is, to borrow a phrase from James Mackaye, a process

of assigning a mark or name to something to which there is occasion to attend. It goes from the thing to the word, not in the reverse direction.

3. By the stipulative substitution of a word for a phrase, language is abbreviated. What can now be said could also have been said previously, without using the new rule or the new name; but it can now be said in fewer words, because the thing can now be indicated by a single name, whereas formerly a descriptive phrase was required. The value of such timesaving does not lie merely or mainly in leaving more time for other activities. Abbreviation not merely shortens discourse; it also increases understanding. We grasp better what we can hold in one span of attention, and how much we can thus hold depends on the length of the symbols we have to use in order to state it. Abbreviations often immensely increase our ability to understand and deal with a subject. The favoured example of this is the shortness of mathematical symbols, from the simple abbreviation of 'III' into '3' to much greater compressions.

4. The greatest good to be obtained by stipulative definitions, however, is different from and much more important than any yet mentioned. It is the improvement of concepts or the creation of new concepts, which is the key to one of the two or three locks on the door of successful science. The notions summoned and held in mind by ordinary words, though rich in suggestions and poetry and emotions, and valuable for their suppleness and ease, have, owing to their vagueness and ambiguity, two defects that make them incapable of establishing science. Neither their applications nor their logical consequences are clear enough. The common word 'hot' is not precise enough for all men to agree on all its applications. There are far too many states of far too many things which one man says are hot and another says are not hot. To make a science having reference to the occurrences commonly called 'hot', we must to some extent turn our backs on the lexical definition of 'hot' and stipulate instead an arbitrary definition of 'temperature'. What we aim at in such a stipulation is that, without losing all touch with common heat, we may arrive at a concept and a word about whose application there will be no doubt and no dis-

agreement. The stipulation of what is to be meant by 'one degree of temperature Centigrade' is of this kind and secures this enormous advantage. The attempt to make psychology a successful science is confronted by the fact that the psychological terms of everyday life are uncertain in their application. We doubt and disagree whether a given behaviour of a given animal is or is not a case of 'shame', or 'intelligence', or 'instinct'. We need to invent new terms, about whose application there will be no doubt, and which will nevertheless have some reference to our abiding interests in such matters as 'intelligence' and 'shame'. So it is everywhere that a body of systematic and successful doctrine has grown up.

At first it does not occur to people to start by getting terms on whose application there will be universal agreement. Instead they spend their time arguing whether 'this is T', that is, whether the term 'T' applies to the given object. The process of criticizing the term 'T', and redefining it by stipulation into something whose applications will not admit of argument, appears to them perverse and useless: useless, because what they want to establish is whether this is a case of 'T' in the ordinary sense; and perverse, because everyone knows perfectly well what 'T' means. John Locke observed that it is a frequent mistake to believe that 'the significations of common words are certainly established, and the precise ideas they stand for certainly known; and . . . it is a shame to be ignorant of them'.[1] He was once present, he tells us, at a meeting of physicians arguing whether a liquor flows along the nerves. To him the argument appeared to arise from the ambiguities of the word 'liquor'; but his fellow practitioners found it an odd suggestion that they should stop to consider what they meant by this word.[2] Such resistance of our common instinct to the first requisite of science never dies. The scientist is still saying 'it depends what you mean by . . .', and the layman is still resenting that answer.

This use of stipulative definition, a sort of turning our backs to reality in order to approach it again with a new set of conceptions that will give us a better grasp of the facts, is part of a more general characteristic of successful science,

[1] *Essay,* III xi. 25.   [2] Ibid. III ix. 16.

its abstractness and hypotheticalness. The axiom, that a body acted on by no force continues moving in the same direction with the same speed for ever, is about something that never has happened and never will happen. That the success of Galileo's mechanics compared with Aristotle's is largely due to the very much greater concreteness of Aristotle, is a point most interestingly brought out by Dr. Drabkin in the *American Journal of Philology* for 1938.

5. We do not speak of 'science' until we have not merely achieved universally accepted descriptions of what we observe, but also subsumed these descriptions under a system about whose logical consequences there is also no doubt. Science requires universal agreement not merely on the applications of its terms to events experienced, but also on the inferences that can be drawn from those terms when they are combined into propositions. Safe and agreed inferences are possible only with precise and unambiguous terms. Thus stipulative definition gives us the immense benefit of certain inference. The outstanding example of this is, of course, mathematics.

The precision and univocity given to concepts by stipulative definition are probably never perfect. It is probably always possible that a vagueness or ambiguity may turn up to-morrow in what now seems a perfectly precise and unambiguous term. This is probably true even within the realm of pure logic and mathematics; but it is more probably true when we are talking about what actually happens. Stipulative definitions in law, or in the contracts of insurance companies, designed to cover events, are always liable to appear inadequate in the light of some new and unforeseen circumstance. Locke hoped too much when he hoped to 'strip all his terms of ambiguity and obscurity'.[1] There can never be 'a flag code that would not be open to various interpretations', as a commander in the American Legion once demanded.

6. It is a false proposition that 'there was a reigning king of France in 1940'. This false proposition is implied in the description 'the man who was king of France in 1940'. If there were a single word that meant the same as this descrip-

[1] *Essay*, III xi. 7.

tion, if, for example, we defined the word 'Grat' to mean the man who was king of France in 1940, the false proposition would be implied in this single word. In this way most descriptive words are compressed or implied propositions, and have the truth or falsity proper to the corresponding propositions. The word 'moon', for instance, implies that there are astronomical bodies revolving round other bodies which in turn revolve round a sun.

When a word comes to be believed to imply a false proposition, as the words 'centaur' and 'phlogiston' are now believed to do, either of the following things may be done with it. (1) It may be retained as the name of a recognized error, as has happened to these two words. But (2) it may be redefined to mean something true and yet closely allied to the original false meaning. The word 'poetry', as commonly used, implies the falsehood that the most profound and noble imaginative literature must always be in verse. Consequently, something needs to be done about this word. In the following passage Edmund Wilson is in doubt whether we should (1) abandon it, or (2) stipulate a new definition for it.

'Surely it is time to discard the word "poetry" or to define it in some different way, so as to recognize the fact that the most intense, the most profound, the most comprehensive, and the most beautifully composed works of literary art (which for these reasons are also the most thrilling and give us most prickly sensations while shaving) have been written sometimes in prose and sometimes in verse, depending chiefly on which literary technique happened to be dominant during the period.'[1]

The word 'simultaneous' and the phrase 'at the same time' have lately been discovered to imply a falsehood, to our considerable astonishment, namely, that the temporal relation of any two events is always independent of anything spatial. But in this case it is obvious that we cannot merely discard this language, because it is indispensable to common life; and Einstein has given us a redefinition to remove the error. For all we know to the contrary, a further error may in the future appear in this or any other word.

[1] 'Is Verse a Dying Technique?', in *The Triple Thinkers*.

Thus it is a sixth use of stipulation, and a very great one, to remove an element of error from a useful word.

Owing to all these advantages that may be secured by stipulation, while, on the other hand, stipulation is not restricted by any considerations of truth and falsity, since it has no truthvalue, the doctrine is often announced that stipulation is free. Pascal wrote that *les définitions sont très-libres*. He was explicitly confining his attention to nominal definitions, and implicitly or unconsciously considering only such nominal definitions as are stipulative. James Mackaye wrote that 'any person is free to stipulate any meaning he pleases for a word and his meaning shall always be accepted'.[1] Making a particular demand under this general principle, J. S. Mill wrote of 'the right I claim for every author, to give whatever provisional definition he pleases of his own subject'.[2] Humpty Dumpty claimed the most entire freedom to give any meaning to any word.

There is much justice in this claim. It is a slogan suggesting many of those truths about words which the linguistic layman ignores or denies. It includes the assertion that stipulation has no truthvalue, which we have seen to be roughly true; stipulation is free in that no stipulative definition can justly be rejected on the ground that it is false. It is also a proper protest against the pedantic grammarian's demand that we should always use our words in the same senses as Samuel Johnson or some other 'authority', and never in any sense not found in the *Oxford English Dictionary*. It is a proper protest against all tyrannous demands, from whatever source, that insist upon everybody's using a word in a particular sense, such as may be seen most months in letters to the newspapers. It suggests a proper protest against the layman's assumption that common meanings are known and clear, and that there is some one 'correct' meaning for each word, in contrast to which all other meanings that may be given to it are 'incorrect'. It upholds the ancient truth, which it goes so much against our grain to believe, that words are conventional not natural signs, that there is no necessary or natural connexion between a word and a thing, no 'predestined' meaning for a given word, as Mac-

[1] *The Logic of Language*, p. 61.   [2] *A System of Logic*, p. 3.

kaye puts it, no sacredness or divine authority about any rule of meaning. It is a just protest against the inability to contemplate the possibility that what one has always meant by some word does not exist, the possibility, for example, that there cannot be such a thing as one has always meant by 'murder', or 'virtue', or 'responsibility', because one has included in one's meaning an uncausedness that does not exist, or that what one has always thought one meant by 'simultaneous' is something that can never be demonstrated to occur, whereas by stipulating a new definition we can make simultaneity into an empirical property. It is a just protest against the common habit of insisting on the question 'But what really *is x*?' even after it has been shown that '*x*' is an ambiguous or vague or inapplicable word.

Nor is the truth of the slogan that 'stipulation is free' at all threatened by the fact that, as logicians say, it is not possible to define certain terms on the basis of certain others.[1] These two statements are not contrary. The first means that you may select any word you like to be the sign of a given concept; and the second means that, when you try to tell other people what selection you have made, you will not be able to do so by referring to any concept you like.

The greatest justification of the doctrine that stipulation is free is that it includes the claim for the right to that redefinition of concepts which is essential to science. There can be no sure and far-reaching control and prediction of events on the basis of the vague and shifting words and notions of ordinary life. We must be released from the lexical definitions which merely describe common usage in all its unscientific nature, and allowed to stipulate simpler, more precise, and more univocal words and ideas, if we are to have science. And this most beneficial freedom is asserted, though in too sweeping a manner, by the doctrine that stipulative definition is free.

On the other hand, a few examples will show that there must be something wrong with the unrestricted doctrine that stipulation is free.

1. A philosopher advertised a lecture on 'The Speculative Use of Language'. As this was during the period when

---

[1] e.g. Carnap, *Introduction to Semantics*, p. 69.

metaphysics was under heavy attack from the positivists, other philosophers inferred that he was going to discuss the justification of metaphysics, and chose to attend or not according as they wished or not to hear another treatment of this subject. The speaker in his opening words explained that he was using the word 'speculative' to mean pictorial, and the whole of his talk concerned the pictorial use of language. He said nothing about metaphysics. Some of his hearers felt that they had been deceived. Aristoxenus tells us that Aristotle used to say that some of the hearers of Plato's lecture on the good felt that they had been deceived in this way.[1] I think that on reflection we should all agree that we have no right to use words in novel senses when advertising a lecture.

2. James Mackaye, in claiming freedom for stipulation, says that John Locke had a perfect right to stipulate that the word 'idea' in his *Essay* was to mean whatever is the object of a man's thoughts when he thinks. Yet there appears to be a very close connexion between this definition and the characteristic defect of Locke's theory of knowledge, namely, the tendency to solipsism inherent in the representative theory of perception. In common use in Locke's century the word 'idea' meant, as it does in ours, something essentially part of the thinker or perceiver and not of the objects he surveys. To redefine it, therefore, as any object of thinking was either to make a most violent departure from usage or to imply that no man can ever think about anything that is not a part of himself. The latter is what happened to Locke, without his intending it. He intended to use the word 'idea' as a mere label indicating that the thing so labelled was an object of someone's thinking. But as it turned out he did not succeed in ridding himself of the customary sense according to which an idea is an event in the human mind. It followed that every object of someone's thinking (Locke's new sense) was an event in the thinker's mind (old customary sense). Thus the result of his stipulation was a gross falsehood. This surely justifies a doubt whether stipulation ought to be entirely free.

3. In his *Theory of the Leisure Class*, a book which has

---

[1] *Harmonics*, II 30–1.

influenced a great many intellectuals, Thorstein Veblen stipulated a special sense for the word 'waste', in order to use it in describing the behaviour of the rich. He wrote that the emotion of disapproval carried by the word in common usage was to be discarded, and the word was to carry only the scientific sense which he assigned to it.

'The use of the term "waste" is in one respect an unfortunate one. As used in the speech of everyday life the word carries an undertone of deprecation. It is here used for want of a better term that will adequately describe the same range of motives and of phenomena, and it is not to be taken in an odious sense.'[1]

In what follows, however, the usual emotion of disapproval continues to attach to the word; and the book, while full of good observations, is much more of a sarcastic attack on the rich than a dispassionate scientific description of them. It is a sarcastic attack on the rich which derives part of its force from penetrating observation and part from pretending to be pure observation without emotional colour. Great numbers of Veblen's immature readers fail to see through the pretence and take the book as pure science, an impression which they retain for life because they never re-read it at a more critical age. Whether Veblen himself was aware of the deception would need a biographical study to determine; but in his book on university education the passion and invective are much less disguised.

Evidently there is something undesirable about this kind of stipulation.

4. For a fourth and last example, if stipulation is perfectly free, why is Humpty Dumpty's procedure in *Alice through the Looking-glass* a laughable absurdity? He seems to be merely exercising the entire freedom of stipulation which some logicians think ought to be accorded to everyone. Is Alice unreasonable in her mild disapproval?

Let us try to state the sorts of limitation that must be put on the doctrine that stipulation is free. They are two, those arising from the fact that stipulation may be used for bad purposes, and those arising from the fact that stipulation, whatever its purpose, has unintended consequences, some of which are bad.

[1] *Theory of the Leisure Class*, p. 97.

The advantages of stipulation already recited are all advantages of which on reflection we approve. The advantages secured by stipulation may, however, also be of a sort we disapprove. Such are the following:

1. Stipulation may be used to induce people to attend a lecture or buy a book which they would otherwise disregard, by using in the title a word that customarily means something interesting to them, and then explaining in the work that you have stipulated some other meaning for it. Thus by 'light verse' most people understand gay and humorous verse; but, if they buy W. H. Auden's *Oxford Book of Light Verse* on this assumption, they read:

'When the things in which the poet is interested, the things which he sees about him, are much the same as those of his audience, and that audience is a fairly general one, he will not be conscious of himself as an unusual person, and his language will be straightforward and close to ordinary speech . . . ⟨and⟩ his poetry will be "light" in the sense in which it is used in this anthology. . . . Light verse can be serious, ⟨but cannot be difficult. Burns and Byron are light poets.⟩'

And so they find among the poems included 'Mary weeps for her Child', 'Matthew Mark Luke and John', and Housman's bitter 'The Laws of God, the Laws of Man'.

2. From its use in science, stipulation acquires some of the prestige of science. It can therefore be used to impress the hearer or reader with the importance or scientificalness of the stipulator. This seems to be the only advantage which Humpty Dumpty could possibly achieve by his stipulations, and the only advantage of the following stipulation in the title of an article in a scientific journal: 'Geophagy (Dirt Eating) among Mississippi Negro School Children.'[1] The word 'geophagy' has to be immediately explained by a word that is in no way inferior to it in precision or applicability or intelligibility, and has the great advantage of being far better known. The sole reason for introducing 'geophagy' seems to be the hope of overawing the layman.

3. Whether or not Veblen was conscious of his purpose, his purpose in stipulating a special meaning for 'waste' was to make use of the ordinary meaning of the word, including its emotional force, and to heighten its effect by giving it an

[1] *American Sociological Review*, 1942.

air of scientific detachment. It was a case of having it both ways, of disclaiming but nevertheless using the common meaning; and this is a very common purpose of stipulation. It is no doubt occasionally conscious, but far more often unconscious. It arises very easily because it is not possible to cancel the ingrained emotion of a word merely by an announcement. Nothing but a completely new context well sustained will achieve it, and then only slowly. We may nearly say that the emotional dimension of meaning is not amenable to redefinition by stipulation; only the descriptive dimension is so. One cannot stipulate that this word is to carry this emotion and is no longer to carry that emotion. More accurately, one can stipulate it, but one's stipulation usually has no more effect even on one's own usage than Canute had on the waves.

The possibility, then, of these bad purposes to which stipulation may be put shows clearly that there are limits to the extent to which stipulation is free. This freedom is further limited by the bad consequences which may follow from a stipulation, apart from the author's conscious or un-conscious purpose in making the stipulation.

4. Let us notice first one such bad consequence that is closely related to the last of our three bad purposes. The illicit survival of the old sense after its supposed replacement by a new one may occur, we have said, on purpose. But it may also occur entirely apart from the author's purposes and to their detriment. That is the important fact displayed in Locke's treatment of the word 'idea'. From the fact that a man at the beginning of his book stipulates in good faith that a certain word is to be understood in a certain sense throughout the work, it does not follow with a high degree of probability that the word is so and only so used. Some-thing happens to us when we write. Using a word always in a particular artificial sense is not an automatic consequence of stipulating that sense. It is something that has to be procured by labour. It is something that the word in its customary sense often strenuously and secretly resists. One may argue with some plausibility that stipulation is foolish because it is pretty certain that we shall not perform what we promise. We shall use the word in senses other than the

stipulated one, because we cannot foresee or call to mind all the uses we habitually have for that word, or the new uses that may suddenly arise. In the struggle to make or express ideas, we may at any time be suddenly and irresistibly led to a new usage. To obtain or express new insight into reality requires us to use words in all sorts of ways, and not to be bound by any stipulation.

5. Stipulations are an extra labour to make and to read. In stipulating we abandon the ease and obviousness of customary speech, and compel ourselves and our hearers to use a foreign language. Stipulation puts upon the speaker the labour of making a new rule of meaning instead of using an old one. It puts upon the hearer the strain of learning and remembering a new rule of meaning. It lengthens discourse by adding to the substantive sentences other sentences about the words used in the substantive sentences, which would have been unnecessary if the substantive sentences had been composed of ordinary words in ordinary senses. This extra labour is usually good for one book only. The next book stipulates a different set of usages. In these ways stipulation violates Schopenhauer's sound maxim that a writer should make a sparing use of his reader's time, patience, and attention. From this point of view Mackaye's statement, 'Any person is free to stipulate any meaning he pleases for a word and his meaning shall always be accepted', is like saying 'Any person is free to talk any language he likes to me and I am always obliged to listen to him for as long as he wishes to talk'.

6. Stipulation usually uglifies discourse. Strange usages and new terms are more often ugly than beautiful. 'Nondenumerable' and 'psychoanalysis' and 'E-boat' and such are words without charm. But it is a duty, though not, of course, a paramount duty, to produce beauty rather than ugliness at all times and places.

7. The habit of stipulating one's own meaning for words tends to bring with it the habit of evading the analysis of obscure conceptions and the clarification of actual meanings. Here lies the reason for the opposition between those thinkers who freely stipulate new meanings and those who hold firmly to customary meanings. The former think that the custo-

mary meanings are vague and confused. The latter think that the customary meanings suggest important truths which we overlook if, like the mathematician, we stipulate our own meanings and turn our backs on reality. (A striking example of these opposed tendencies is the treatment of probability by Keynes and by von Mises. Keynes is piously inclined towards the customary meaning of 'probable'. He tries to analyse it and build on it. Von Mises, however, completely turns his back on common usage and starts afresh with an arbitrarily and carefully stipulated definition of his own.) Both sides are right. Our business at the moment is to insist on the rightness of those who preserve customary meanings, in order to show the dangers of stipulation. It is quite necessary, for example, to analyse what we really mean in common language by 'right' and 'good' and 'just' and 'value', and not merely to stipulate some meanings of our own invention for these words because they are clearer and easier to work with. In logic the work of the last half-century has shown clearly that it is quite necessary to analyse what we actually mean by 'implication', and not merely to turn our backs on ordinary implication and consider only some newly stipulated meaning for the word. In other words, the habit of stipulative definition tends to weaken the habit of real definition, tends in fact to lead to the assertion that real definition is a mere mistake; and I hope my chapter on real definition will show that this is an exaggeration.

8. Abbreviation, the replacement of a phrase by a name, involves the disappearance of words reminding us of the complexity of a thing. Most names, whether names of simple or of complex objects, fail to mirror by their structure any complexity in the object. The complex of letters and syllables in the word 'raglan' is not a reflection of any complexity there may be in the thing it means. To abbreviate a phrase into a word, therefore, is always to set up a cause that may lead men to overlook an important complexity or relation, or to find mystery where there is none. He who forgets that 'five' is an abbreviation for 'one and one and one and one and one', and similarly with other names for numbers, may find it mysterious and wonderful that seven plus five must equal twelve.

Since then stipulation has bad effects as well as good, and is therefore not entirely free, can we give ourselves rules to follow in order to secure more of its good and less of its bad results?

§ 4. Rules for Stipulative Definition. The above discussion of the advantages and disadvantages of stipulation suggests certain rules of stipulation that we may usefully lay upon ourselves.

In the first place, certain rules emerge from the previous discussion without need of much further argument.

1. The supreme rule of stipulation is surely to *stipulate as little as possible.* Do not change received definitions when you have nothing to complain of in them, says the Port Royal Logic. And the reason for it is that stipulation as such is sure to do some harm and is not sure to do any good. It is sure to do some harm because it is a destruction of custom or at least a going outside custom, and this always makes for awkwardness and ugliness and failures of communication. It sometimes does good which outweighs the harm; but whether it does so is always a matter for careful reflection in the particular case. Dozens of would-be scientific writers are unreadable and unread to-day merely because of unrestrained stipulation. We should scrutinize our stipulations after we have made them to see whether they have really been useful, whether they have really done more good than harm. The next four rules, nos. 2–5, are mostly applications of this supreme rule.

2. Everything can already be referred to by phrases or at any rate by sentences, but not everything can already be referred to by a single word; that is, not everything has a name. The question whether to stipulate is therefore often the question whether we must have a name for a certain thing, or can get along well enough with the phrase that already exists for it. This indicates the rule: *Let us not stipulate until we have good reason to believe that the phrase which already covers our designatum is too cumbrous for our purposes.*

Humpty Dumpty stipulates a new meaning and uses it once only. He is like a man who, wishing to say that the sky is overcast, says instead: 'By "soda" I shall mean that the sky is overcast. Soda.' He uses eleven words to say what four would say better, and these four are included in his eleven.

We cannot, however, lay down the principle that it is always bad to stipulate a usage that is to be used once only. It often happens that a complicated statement can be better understood if one phrase in it is replaced by a single symbol, and this symbol is stipulatively defined, for this occasion only, in the next sentence. We often find it easier to grasp a shorter sentence plus the special definition of one of its symbols, than to grasp a longer sentence with everything written out and no attached definition. Even for a single use, therefore, it may be good to stipulate a name. But the weaker principle remains, that we should not stipulate unless we have good reason to believe that the phrase already covering our designatum is too cumbrous for our purpose.

3. *Let us not stipulate until we have good reason to believe that there is no name for the thing we wish to name.* Stipulation has become so common and attractive nowadays that many writers tend to invent a name if they cannot dig one out of their own memories by a day's reflection. But it is not sufficient to consult one's memory. It is required to consult also the experts, including the experts in those fields of study which the accidents of contemporary departmentalization separate from one's own. It often happens that, say, a philosopher invents a new term to name something for which, say, the lawyers have long had an agreed term. Professor Dubs illustrates the violation of this rule by the definition of 'evolution' as 'a directional change with a transition to novelty'; for that, he points out, is just what the word 'change' already means.[1]

4. *Let us not stipulate two different symbols to mean the same thing*, since evidently this doubles the bad results without increasing the good results. If the reader is inclined to disbelieve that any writer ever does this, he will find on p. 438 of *Purposive Behavior in Animals and Men* that one of Professor E. C. Tolman's new formations, 'behavior-feint', is explicitly defined to mean the same as another of his new formations, 'behavior-adjustment'.

5. *Let us not stipulate one symbol for two different things.*

[1] *Philosophical Review*, 1943, pp. 576–7.

This rule is given by Pascal.[1] It is obviously correct, and easy to violate through overlooking an ambiguity in one's method of stipulating, or through overlooking another sense which the word already has. Thus Cohen and Nagel's *Logic* has two senses of 'independent': (1) propositions are independent of each other if neither implies the truth of the other; (2) propositions are independent of each other if neither the truth nor the falsity of one implies either the truth or the falsity of the other. They use the first sense in discussing postulates, and the second in discussing the various possibilities of implication among any pair of propositions.

6. *Let us not attempt to change the emotional force of a word by stipulation.* The result, as we have seen in Veblen's 'waste', is almost bound to be a failure, and is likely to be a deception as well. The emotional powers of language are open to man's manipulation only partially and indirectly, much like a living plant. There is no question of changing a potato into a tomato at will. This is why literary as opposed to scientific writers are against stipulation. They deal largely in the emotional powers of language, and they know that these cannot be controlled by stipulation. They know the falsity of their own words: 'What's in a name? That which we call a rose by any other name would smell as sweet.' The most that stipulation can do here is to direct the emotional force of a word upon a new object by redefining the descriptive force of the word.

7. In general, we should *make sure that our stipulation is not a deception and will not deceive*, or at least that the likelihood of its deceiving someone is strongly outweighed by the good it will do.

The above rules follow rather closely from our discussion of the advantages and disadvantages of stipulation. I come now to some further rules that also seem desirable.

8. It seems useful to warn ourselves against stipulating degenerate meanings for words. A redefinition of a word degenerates it if it leaves us bereft of any means of indicating an important distinction that could be indicated by the word in its previous sense. Professor Malcolm, to whom I largely

[1] *L'Esprit de la Géometrie*, p. 281, in Vol. II of Havet's edition of the *Pensées*. He has other rules for stipulation, pp. 301–2.

owe this conception, points out[1] in effect that the redefinition of a 'certain' empirical statement as a highly probable empirical statement, which is often urged to-day, leaves us without any word to describe the obvious difference between thinking it highly probable that Joe Louis won the fight last night, because of the past performances of himself and his opponent, and thinking it 'certain' that he did so, because the newspapers and the eyewitnesses all say so. Similarly the doctrine that all actions are selfish, which amounts to redefining 'selfish' action as action aimed at the doer's own purposes, leaves us without a word for distinguishing those obviously distinct persons, the man whose purpose is usually a pleasant state of his own body or mind, and the man whose purpose is usually a pleasant state of some other persons' bodies or minds. For a third example, the following passage attacks the view that Plato's theory of method was not empirical by implicitly redefining 'empirical' so that all attempts to know any truth are empirical by definition, a procedure which renders 'empirical' a useless word, because it no longer distinguishes some methods from others.

'The author says of Plato in the *Phaedo* that "he never thinks of an empirical test; the whole inquiry is by discussion merely". But has anyone ever engaged seriously in a discussion which was not *about* some empirical fact? As Plato maintains in the *Sophist*, it is impossible that there should be a logos which is not the logos *of* something. Hence any logos, by its very nature, is constantly submitting itself to an empirical test by constantly confronting itself with that rational object *of* which it is the logos. It is therefore true . . . that no *special* effort to return to experience for an empirical test is to be found in the writings of Plato. We cannot divide them into an empirical part and a non-empirical part. This is because Plato never divided himself from experience in the first place.'[2]

On the usage here implied, all attempts whatever to say anything true are 'empirical', including attempts to say how many planets there are on the basis of whether six or seven is the more perfect number.

9. After such a redefinition of 'empirical' or 'selfish' or 'certain', it is still necessary to use the word occasionally in

---

[1] *Mind*, 1942, pp. 35–6.
[2] *Philosophy and Phenomenological Research*, II 549.

the old sense, because the old sense indicated a distinction that really existed and was very important to us. Thus such a redefinition breaks Professor Stevenson's rule of stipulation that *the new sense must make it unnecessary ever to use the old sense.*[1] A redefinition of an unclear term is not good, he declares, unless it enables men to say all that they in future want to say without ever going back to the earlier sense of the word. Are we to accept this rule?

So far as I can see, the rule should be accepted for the sort of case that Professor Stevenson has in mind, namely, a redefinition of a word with the intention of understanding better what one has always been talking about by means of that word. The word he has in mind is 'good'. He rejects any stipulation that takes us right away from what we ordinarily mean by 'good', and seeks for a definition that shall be clearer than our ordinary sense, and yet so close to it that we no longer need the ordinary sense. A similar conception of definition appears in these words by Henry Sidgwick:

'It is an assumption of the Intuitional method that the term "justice" denotes a quality which it is ultimately desirable to realize in the conduct and social relations of men; and that a definition may be given of this which will be accepted by all competent judges as presenting, in a clear and explicit form, what they have always meant by the term, though perhaps implicitly and vaguely. In seeking such a definition we may, so to speak, clip the ragged edge of common usage, but we must not make excision of any considerable portion.'[2]

The kind of definition that Sidgwick here describes is so little stipulative as to be almost historical. Many persons would doubt whether it is possible to give a definition of 'justice' which should both satisfy all our vague meanings and intentions and be clear and consistent. Possibly Sidgwick shared this doubt; for he describes this ideal as 'an assumption of the intuitional method'; and, while believing in the inevitability of intuitions, he rejected most of the characteristic intuitionist method. It is clear, however, that in this kind of stipulation we should aim at preserving as much as possible of the intention and ideal implicit in the ordinary use of the word.

On the other hand, we cannot submit to Professor Steven-

---

[1] *Mind*, 1937, p. 15.   [2] *The Methods of Ethics*, III v 1.

son's rule in every case of redefining an old word; for many such definitions are made with a very special and temporary purpose, and leave the ordinary meanings of the word undisturbed. Thus for the sake of a theory of series a mathematician may stipulate a definition of 'between' that will by no means dispense with all the ordinary senses.

10. Descartes included among his rules of method one calling for *review*; and it seems very useful that, as stipulators, we should lay on ourselves the rule to *make sure that we have used the word as we said we would*. After our writing is finished, we should examine it to see whether those words, for which we stipulated a special sense, are actually used in it in that sense. For nothing is easier than to announce one meaning for a word and then use it in another. Freedom of imposition gives rise to necessity of observance, said Candalla according to Enriques.[1] One freedom that stipulators are certainly not entitled to is the freedom to disregard their own stipulations.

John Stuart Mill in his logic claimed for every author 'the right . . . to give whatever provisional definition he pleases of his own subject'. Can we allow this?

An author usually has a right:

(1) to compose a book on any matter he pleases,

subject to any special obligation that may prevent him in a particular case, such as that he does not know the matter well enough to come before the public with it. Less often, but sometimes, an author has the right:

(2) to name his subject by a specially stipulated name of his own.

This second right, however, is often cancelled by the intervention of the fact that no author ever has a right:

(3) to give, at the beginning of his book, a false impression of what it is about.

He can always read his book after he has written it, and discover what it is about, and then correct any false account of it that he may have given in his first chapter before the rest was written. It is his duty to do this, and to remove from his introduction all 'provisional' statements he may have

[1] *The Historic Development of Logic*, New York, 1929, p. 72.

made about the contents of his book, if the actual writing
has failed to bear them out. Mill's remark, on the contrary,
seems to be claiming that an author has the right to publish
his introduction as he first wrote it even if the subsequent
chapters falsify it. (He does, however, go on to say that in
his case the provisional definition turns out to be also final.)

11. Should we banish all privately stipulated senses of
words from our titles, and declare that *words in titles should
always bear their customary senses*?

The chief purpose of a title is to be a name to use in
referring to the work. To fulfil this purpose a title need have
no previous significance whatever, as the word 'Piccadilly'
in the twentieth century fulfils the purpose of being the name
of a street while conveying nothing else (except the associations of that street so named). Almost always, however, the
title of a work of art or science is not merely a label, but also
consists of words conveying a customary meaning. It seems,
then, that this meaning ought not to give a false impression
of the nature of the work. However, it makes a great difference whether the work is scientific or artistic. The title of
an artistic work might be a necessary part of the whole
artistic effect; and its value as such might outweigh its causing false expectations. On this ground there may be a justification for giving a name like 'Man with Dog' to a painting
that appears to represent nothing. Possibly this may even
justify the act of publishing an artistic fiction in such a way
as to make people think it is history. The hardest species
to justify in this class would be the misleading title given to
a film or play or pageant or other artistic event occurring
rarely and costing much time and trouble and some money
to attend.

In all works whose purpose is descriptive rather than
artistic, on the other hand, it seems evident that the title
should be carefully chosen to give prospective readers the
best idea of what is in the work *before* they read it. It should
not be dismissed by saying: 'This is only a matter of words.
I have a right to choose these topics for discussion if I wish,
and the title is quite a minor consideration.'[1] Dr. Ewing

---

[1] A. C. Ewing, *Idealism*, p. 6.

has a right to choose his topics, but no right to give them
a title that would lead buyers to think they were getting
a discussion of some other topic. Not that he has done so
in this work; his title is as good an indication of its contents
as could be found.

This rule is less obligatory, however, the more oppor-
tunity our clients have of learning the nature of our medicine
before swallowing it. It is most obligatory when we are
giving an oral lecture or speech or sermon for a single time.
An author should write, or at least reconsider, his title *after*
he has finished his work and knows what he *has* written as
opposed to what he *expected* to write.

12. The obvious but often forgotten rule, that we should
get friends to criticize, should always be applied to stipulations
as to all writing. Faraday opens one of his famous discussions of electrolysis with a section on definitions. In order
to make his points he finds it almost essential to stipulate
some new terms; but he is apologetic about doing so, and
tells us that he got two friends to help him with the definitions. Professor Dubs writes that 'editors and reviewers
should police philosophical writings; any article failing to
define its terms clearly or unnecessarily departing from
established meanings of words should be considered unworthy
of being offered to the public'.

13. When we need a name for something which has
previously not had a name, is it better to invent a new word
or to use an old word in the new sense? Is it better, for
example, to call a new weapon of war a 'bazooka' (assuming
this to be a new sound) or to call it a 'tank', using an old
word in a new sense?

On the one hand, Professor Dubs writes: 'Since there
are far more concepts than words, the scientist can only use
an old word with a new meaning.' And he mentions 'salt'
as an example.

On the other hand, A. E. Housman said in his lecture on
The Name and Nature of Poetry:

'We should beware of treating the word poetry as chemists have
treated the word salt. Salt is a crystalline substance recognised by its
taste; its name is as old as the English language and is the possession of
the English people, who know what it means: it is not the private

property of a science less than three hundred years old, which, being in want of a term to embody a new conception, "an acid having the whole or part of its hydrogen replaced by a metal", has lazily helped itself to the old and unsuitable word salt, instead of excogitating a new and therefore to that extent an apt one. The right model for imitation is that chemist who . . . invented out of his own head . . . the useful word *gas*.'

Professor Dubs's statement that the scientist *can* only use an old word with a new meaning is clearly a mistake. It is quite easy to invent a sound which carries no meaning to the majority of English-speakers. It is quite easy also to invent a sound which, while suggesting another sound that already is a sign, is so altered as to be clearly intended as a new word. Scientists have done the latter thousands of times. Recent examples are 'matterism' for a view distinct from materialism but close to it, and 'penicillin' for a product of penicillium. The former, however, is rarely done; and the conscious stipulator feels a strong reluctance to do it, although it is perfectly possible. Housman writes as if he believed that the words 'gas' and 'manna' were invented as purely arbitrary combinations of phonemes; but according to the *Oxford English Dictionary* 'gas' was formed from 'chaos', to mean a state of matter in which the arrangement of the particles was chaotic; and the author of the article on manna in Hastings's *Dictionary of the Bible* thinks that 'manna' too was not a perfectly new sound when the Israelites made it the name of their god-sent food, though he is not confident what it had previously meant. So that here too the stipulator was not creating a new sound wholly unrelated to existing signs. The psychological causes of this reluctance would be worth investigating.

We may now restate our question in terms of three alternatives instead of two: Should the person who is giving a name to a hitherto unnamed object choose:

(1) an old word,

or (2) a new word recognizably constructed out of old words,

or (3) a new word having no relation to existing words?

It appears that none of these three alternatives is always bad and to be avoided. The first of them, the use of an old word in a new sense, adds to the ambiguity of language; and

Housman's blame of it is partly justified. Yet any reader of scientific works can think of cases where it has been chosen and was obviously the correct choice. It is sometimes the correct choice when the nominand is a special case of something more vague or general that already has a name. Thus Professor Price on *Perception* distinguishes two features of perception to which he gives the names 'acceptance' and 'assurance'. These are objects previously unnamed, but so closely related to the ordinary meanings of these words, in the peculiar relation of the precise to the vague, that it would have been much less suitable to invent new words for them.

The following defence of the first procedure occurs in Mr. G. D. H. Cole's *Money*:

'Those writers whose business is with the affairs of everyday life are often placed, in this respect, in a peculiar difficulty. They cannot without extravagance avoid the use of everyday terms which are full of associative significance and are in many cases used in different senses in different connections. They have, however, to give to these words meanings more fixed and more precise than are given to them in ordinary speech; and, in doing so, they often appear to the layman to be talking nonsense and to be doing violence to the common meaning of ordinary words. Economists are especially liable to this source of misunderstanding.'

To a smaller or greater degree every descriptive writer is in this dilemma. If he uses words in their common meanings he will be somewhat vague and confused. If he uses them in specially stipulated meanings he will be somewhat repellent and somewhat confusing though not himself confused. Accuracy and intelligibility do not vary together. The descriptive writer, that is, the scientist as opposed to the poet, wants both and is therefore always compelled to compromise.

It follows that no hard and fast rule is desirable here. We may think it probable, however, that the first alternative, which is to give the new sense to an old word that already has at least one sense, is chosen too often and the others not often enough. We may also think it probable that the alternative which is oftenest the best is the second, constructing a new word out of old elements. This procedure retains a great deal of the advantage of the first, which is the feeling of familiarity. Yet it avoids creating a new ambiguity and gives clear warning that a new object of thought is being referred to, which is the advantage of the third. And it has its own great advantage, only feebly reproduced in the first and not at all in the third, namely, that it indicates explicitly some important relation of the nominand to other things. 'Penicillin' indicates explicitly that the substance so named is produced by penicillium.

A universal adoption of the second mode of naming would not necessarily cause the average length of words to be always increasing. Language has many devices for shortening itself again, especially when it is not repressed by academicians. Spoken language is always tending to shorten itself to the verge of unintelligibility.

14. When the second or third alternative is chosen, when a new sound is made, whether out of syllables already significant or not, we may safely lay upon ourselves the rule that it should be as beautiful and as much in accord with the spirit of the language as possible. But what is beauty in words? And what is the spirit of a given language? The pronouncements sometimes uttered by eminent writers, to the effect that (say) 'silver' is the most beautiful word in the English language, proceed from personal experiences and have no general validity. Nor is the spirit of a language, as Wilhelm von Humboldt seems to have thought, anything determined by the blood of its speakers. Human speech in general is largely controlled and directed by the shape of the interior parts of the human head and neck; but this is common to all languages and does not determine what is peculiar to any. The spirit peculiar to a particular language is determined not at all by heredity (by 'heredity' I mean what is fixed for a man before his birth) but entirely by the cultural environment to which its speakers are exposed after their birth, and which they in turn help to make for the next generation. A large part of the generally valid beauty of words is their mere familiarity and the associations that grow on the familiar. Such beauty the newly invented word of course cannot have, while on the other hand it would be foolish to reject all inventions on this ground, since they will seem just as beautiful on this account to our posterity as any word a century old may seem to ourselves. But there is a certain very

important beauty or ugliness that the newly invented word can have at once, and that is its agreement or disagreement with the prevailing habits of pronunciation and syllabification and the prevailing preferences as to length and form. 'Insouciance', for example, is an ugly word in English because if pronounced French fashion it contains sounds not in the English alphabet, while if we try to pronounce it English fashion we discover that there is no English way of pronouncing 'ouci'. 'Schizophrenia' is an ugly word in English because no ordinary Englishman can pronounce it without feeling that perhaps he ought to have pronounced it some other way. 'Ps-' as the beginning of a syllable is contrary to English habits of syllabification, and consequently all words formed from the Greek 'psyche' are ugly in English except so far as we can ignore the 'p'.

There are many points on which the spirit of English is unknown even to the most objective and advanced students of the language. This is sometimes because the spirit differs in different English-speaking societies. Sometimes it is because we cannot tell whether a new phenomenon is a temporary aberration or the beginning of a great change. Sometimes it is because English is in conflict with itself, or vacillating. For example, is it the spirit of English to differentiate the nominal and adjectival forms, to talk about 'the sex of bees' but 'the sexual life of bees'; or is it the spirit of English to approximate the noun and adjective forms and talk about 'the sex of bees' and 'the sex life of bees'? Edward Sapir's discussion of 'Whom did you see?' in his *Language* gives a most enjoyable insight into this sort of fact.

Where there is disagreement about the spirit of English, there will be disagreement about the best form for a new word. Each stipulator should form his new word with regard to what he believes to be the spirit of English; and he should inform himself of the spirit of English so far as it can be objectively ascertained. In doing this he will have to detect and disregard many special pleaders and authoritarians and snobs, some of them persons of great learning of the wrong kind.

15. In general, lastly, we may remind ourselves to be *responsible in stipulation*. We should consider what hangs on

our stipulations in the way of good or bad consequences to human knowledge and communication and to our language as a tool of human knowledge and communication and emotion and enjoyment. Perhaps we ought not to stipulate unless we are in some sense authorities in the field to discuss which we stipulate. But here 'field' must not be confined to the recognized areas of study assigned to one 'chair' in a university. Any man who sees some new point, however small, is an authority on that point. Furthermore, the recognized authorities often stipulate very badly. It was bad of the physicians, for example, to use the phrase 'compound fracture' to mean a broken bone that has pierced the skin, since this phrase so strongly suggests another injury, namely, a double break or the breaking of two bones. It is bad of the lexicographers to use 'primary sense' to mean the earliest sense of a word, since this term strongly suggests to the layman that it is the sense he himself *ought* to use.[1]

Yet the need for authoritative stipulation is great, because the need for agreed stipulation is great, and agreement upon arbitrary matters can come only through authority. This need is felt most by the biologists, who therefore have gone farthest in setting up authorities to standardize names. For example, there is an International Commission on Zoological Nomenclature, which maintains rules of nomenclature, but also has plenary powers to break these rules if it sees fit. In 1944 it was considering using these powers to keep the customary name of a malarial parasite although this name was contrary to the rules.[2] Probably many other groups, such as manufacturers, would profit greatly by imitating the biologists more than they do. When there is an authority, stipulations lose their defect of being good for one book only. We ought, therefore, in deciding whether to stipulate, always to have an eye to the possible or actual existence of an authority for stipulations in our field.

The justification of all these rules, if they are justified, can only be that the observance of them tends to lessen the disadvantages of stipulation and secure more of the goods which it is fitted to secure.

[1] See Professor Malone's remarks on this point in *Language*, XVI 310–11.
[2] *Science*, 3 November 1944.

METHODS OF WORD-THING DEFINITION

THE most fundamental distinction that can be made with regard to definitions is the distinction between their *purposes* and the *methods* by which they achieve their purposes. One of the possible *purposes* of definition, indicated by the phrase 'word-thing definition', is to report that a certain word means a certain thing, or to secure that it shall mean that thing in future. The three immediately preceding chapters have been a discussion of this purpose, first in general (i.e. Chapter II on word-thing definition), and then in each of its two species in turn (i.e. lexical definition in Chapter III and stipulative definition in Chapter IV). I now turn to consider the *methods* by which the word-thing purpose can be achieved.

The methods of lexical definition and of stipulative definition are fundamentally the same. For the problem, how to indicate a given thing as being the meaning of a given word, is fundamentally the same whether this relation between the word and the thing already exists or is merely proposed for the future. I can therefore discuss the methods of word-thing definition in general. It would be repetitious to discuss first the methods of lexical word-thing definition and afterwards the methods of stipulative word-thing definition. Only occasionally will it be desirable to refer exclusively to one of the species.

§ 0. **There is more than one method.** How is a word-thing definition to be achieved? That is, how can a person teach another person the meaning of a word? We assume that the learner is familiar with the idea of words or symbols in general. We assume that he realizes that this sound which we utter is intended as a word. He knows that it symbolizes something; but he does not yet know what it symbolizes, and we want to tell him. We want to refer him to the thing which is the meaning of this word, in order that he may henceforth connect the two and regard the word as a symbol of the thing. By what methods can this be done?

Method of some sort there must be. That is to say, there

must be something indirect about the procedure. One cannot teach a man the meaning of the word 'wool' by saying: 'The word "wool" means wool, of course!' Word-thing definition is an enterprise which includes referring a man to a thing. The ordinary way of referring a man to a thing is by uttering the name of that thing. But, if he already knows the name of the thing, definition is not needed. Definition is required precisely when he does not yet know its name. The problem of word-thing definition, therefore, is the problem how to refer a man to a thing without using the name of the thing. It is solved when teacher and learner both know that they are thinking of the same thing.

There must be more than one way of achieving word-thing definition. That follows from the fact that in a dictionary some of the explanations can and some cannot be substituted for the word defined. When the dictionary defines 'catalogue' as 'list', we can change 'here is a catalogue' into 'here is a list'. But when it defines 'good' as 'the most general adjective of commendation', we cannot change 'food is good' into 'food is the most general adjective of commendation'.

I shall describe seven different methods of word-thing definition. I do not claim, however, that this division is either exhaustive or exclusive or the only useful one. It is probably not exhaustive, because it is not clear how anyone could be certain that he had given an empirical and yet exhaustive list of the ways of teaching a man the meaning of a word. It is most probably not exclusive; that appears from the fact that many examples of word-thing definition could plausibly be brought under more than one of my heads; and the probable reason for it is that the various ways of defining words form a multidimensional continuum, so that between any two empirically distinguished methods there will be intermediate cases, as there are colours between any two empirically specified colours. My seven methods are merely empirical descriptions of some ways of achieving word-thing definitions which have arisen in human experience and seem at least superficially different. They are a choice of more or less outstanding points in the continuum.

§ 1. **The Method of Synonyms.** There is, first, the *synonymous* method of word-thing definition, which consists in

giving the learner a synonym with which he is already
familiar, that is to say, in telling him that the word being
defined means the same as some other word whose meaning
he already knows. For examples, 'chien' means dog, 'buss'
means kiss.

This is the commonest method in dictionaries, especially
in two-language and in very small one-language dictionaries.
Its brevity and simplicity are useful, and so is its tendency
to reveal or establish a word-for-word correspondence between two languages. But the common doctrine that 'there
are no synonyms' expresses the knowledge that this method
can rarely be practised alone without misleading the learner
to a considerable extent. It deals most successfully, perhaps,
with names of organic kinds: 'Wellingtonia' means Sequoia;
'treecreeper' in So-and-so's book means *Certhia familiaris*.
Dictionaries often seek to overcome its defectiveness by
giving more than one partial synonym, in the hope that the
false in each will be cancelled by the others. Thus a 'catalogue' may be defined as a 'list, register, or complete
enumeration'. But this demands much more previous knowledge of language from the learner than does the pure
method of synonyms. Furthermore, if the word undergoing
definition has any peculiar element in its meaning one cannot
give this peculiarity to the learner merely by removing all
wrong suggestions.

In asserting the possibility of defining by synonyms I
appear to be contradicting the traditional rule, found in
dozens of logic-books, that a definition should contain no
term synonymous with the term being defined. If we take
the traditional rule as referring to nominal definition, it is
obviously false; for obviously we can and do define the word
'buss' by saying 'it means kiss'. But in fact this rule, like all
the traditional rules, was made with real definition in mind.
I discuss the traditional rules in a section at the end of this
chapter.

It may be objected that giving a synonym is not word-
thing definition but word-word definition. In reply to this
I agree that whenever a man gives a synonym he thereby at
the least implies a word-word definition or suggests how one
might be formed. And I also agree that sometimes when

a man gives a synonym his purpose is precisely to make a word-word definition. But I urge that at other times when a man gives a synonym his purpose is to make a word-thing definition. For example, sometimes when a man says that 'valour' means courage his purpose is, not to state the word-word fact that the word 'valour' is equivalent to the word 'courage', but to state the word-thing fact that the word 'valour' means the thing courage. When the hearer already knows the meaning of the word 'courage', and therefore can be referred to the thing courage by the word 'courage', then the word-thing definition of the word 'valour' can be accomplished by the synonymous method.

§ 2. **The Method of Analysis.** It often happens that a man who does not know the name for the thing nevertheless understands a phrase that gives the analysis of the thing. This makes possible a second method of defining words, namely, to refer the learner to the thing meant by giving an *analysis* of it. Thus we may say: 'The word "octagon" means a polygon having eight sides.' The *Oxford English Dictionary*'s definition of a 'list' as 'a catalogue or roll consisting of a row or series of names' proceeds by giving two synonyms for the word followed by an analysis of the thing.

Aristotle's method of defining by genus and differentia, when applied to the definition of words as opposed to things, becomes a case of the analytical method of word-thing definition. To indicate what specific object a word means, name a bigger class within which that object falls, and then name something that distinguishes it from the rest of that class. If man falls within the bigger class of animal, and is distinguished from the rest of that class by rationality, we may define the word 'man' as meaning the rational animal.

In many cases dictionaries content themselves with merely naming the bigger class, and do not say what differentiates the thing meant from the rest of the class. Thus the *Oxford English Dictionary* defines 'gomer' as 'a Hebrew measure', which does not differentiate because there are some Hebrew measures that are not gomers. It also defines 'golland' as 'a name given to various species of *Ranunculus*, *Caltha*, and *Trollius*', abandoning the attempt to say which species of *Ranunculus* are called 'golland'. This is very common, because many words are such that we require much space and labour to give and receive a specific account of their meaning, while a merely general account satisfies most of our needs.

The analytical method is widely felt to be the best of all, and many persons refuse to call an operation 'definition' if it does not proceed by this method. But the nominal purpose, to tell a person the meaning of a word, can certainly be achieved by other methods besides the analytical; and there-fore this restriction can be justified only by regarding our purpose as being not merely to teach a man the meaning of a word but also to teach him the analysis of the thing meant by that word. To confine ourselves to the purpose of con-veying the meaning of a word, and yet insist that this purpose is not to be called 'definition' unless it is achieved by one specific method, is unreasonable.

The great advantage of the analytic method is, of course, that besides letting us know what thing the word means it also gives us an analysis of the thing, which is a most valu-able sort of knowledge.

A disadvantage of the method is that it involves the extra effort of thought required by analysis and synthesis. Com-pared with the method of synonyms, the method of analysis is an elaborate and expensive way of achieving a simple end.

Another disadvantage of the analytical method is that it is not available for all words. It cannot be used for words meaning something that has no analysis or no known analysis. It could not be used to define 'water' before the analysis of water was known. It cannot be used to define 'blue' because no analysis of blue tint is known. It is known that blue is correlated with a certain wavelength (and this is often used to make a synthetic definition of the word 'blue'). It is known that every blue appearance can be analysed into a certain lightness and a certain richness of a certain tint. But the tint itself, any specific blue, has not been analysed and does not look like being so.

The analytical method of definition is usually impossible for words meaning particular things, as 'Julius Caesar' or 'the United Kingdom'. This is because every analysis of Julius Caesar or Big Ben into their specific characteristics gives a complex that could logically belong to some other particular also. This fact is what the traditional logicians had in mind when they said that there was no definition of individuals. If we try to analyse Caesar, in the same way as we analyse man, into a complex of conceptions, animal, rational, bald, and so on, we find that, though we soon reach a complex equivalent to man, we never reach a complex equivalent to Julius Caesar. There is another sort of analysis, however, by which particular things are sometimes analysable, namely, the analysis into physical parts. Thus perhaps it is an accurate definition of the symbol 'United Kingdom' to say it means Scotland plus Northern Ireland plus Wales plus England. But even this sort of analysis is of very limited value for the definition of proper names; for it depends on the learner's being in some way familiar already with the individual parts of the thing meant by the word being defined, and the person who does not know what thing a given proper name refers to is usually unfamiliar with the individual parts of that thing. If we are familiar with an individual or its parts, and there is a name for that individual, we usually know the name. Thus it comes to be very roughly true that the analytical method can define 'bell' but not 'Big Ben', and 'book' but not 'The Bible'.

§ 3. **The Method of Synthesis.** Words may be defined, thirdly, by the *synthetic* method of indicating the relation of the thing they mean to other things.

> '*Feuillemorte*' is the colour of withered leaves in autumn.
> By 'red' people mean those colours which a normal person sees when his eye is struck by light of wavelength 7,000–6,500 A.

A particular colour is here indicated by mentioning where it can be found or what causes it. No synonym is given, nor is the colour analysed. The thing meant is assigned to its place in a system of relations, synthesized into a whole with other things. Whereas the analytic method indicates the thing meant by showing it as a whole of parts, the synthetic does so by showing it as part of a whole.

The *Oxford English Dictionary* defines 'gonidium': 'one of the cells filled with chlorophyll which are formed beneath the cortical layer in the thallus of lichens; now known to be imprisoned algae.' This definition is analytic to the extent that it defines 'gonidium' as meaning an alga-cell filled with chlorophyll, and synthetic in describing this cell as imprisoned with others beneath the cortical layer in the thallus of lichens. In so far as where a thing is found is neither clearly included in nor clearly excluded from the meaning of some word for the thing, it is not clear whether a definition of that word is analytic or synthetic. The word 'mahogany', for example, might be held by some to mean a certain type of wood wherever found, but by others to mean that type of wood only when found in certain species of trees; and then a definition which said that this word was found in such and such species would be regarded as synthetic by one party but as analytic by the other.

Duhamel's dictum, 'The definition of a thing is the expression of its relation to other known things', may be rewritten for our purpose, 'The synthetic method of word-thing definition indicates the thing meant by mentioning its relation to some other known things'. It might therefore be called the 'relational' method of definition. It might also be called the 'locant' method of definition, as defining words by metaphorically placing their significates in a space.

Ogden and Richards in *The Meaning of Meaning* appear to consider the synthetic method as covering all methods of defining words. They regard the method of defining a word as always analogous to the process of telling a man where a place is by describing its spatial connexions with a place he already knows. Since all things are in relations, the thing the word signifies will always be in relations. We define the word, then, by first indicating some starting-point and then indicating a relation that leads from that starting-point to the significate of the word. Thus the method of word-thing definition is always 'locant' according to Ogden and Richards.

A famous sort of synthetic definition is the causal or genetic definition, which indicates the thing signified by mentioning how it is caused or whence it arises. Thus 'circle' may be said to mean the figure covered by a line moving in a plane with one end fixed.

The synthetic method has the great advantage of being theoretically always possible. Everything, we believe, is in a unique relation to other things. Therefore everything could, if we knew enough, be exhibited as the unique term to which a given term is in a given relation. But the analytical and the synonymous methods are not always possible even theoretically, since not everything can be exhibited as a whole of parts, nor has every word a synonym. If there were no methods but the synonymous and the analytical, we should have to admit that some words were indefinable. But words like 'blue', of which there seems to be no analytical definition, are easily defined synthetically by the fixed relations of their significates to other phenomena. And words for particular things are easily defined synthetically by the use of some unique relation in time or place. ' "Big Ben" means the biggest bell in the Houses of Parliament.'

'God is the supreme spirit' is a synthetic definition of a name for a particular thing. The relation of supremacy to all other things determines what is meant. It is like explaining which is John by saying that John is the tallest man in the room. Synthetic or relational definition indicates a particular by mentioning one of its unique relations to another particular.

A further advantage of the synthetic method is that in stipulative definition it sometimes enables us to reach greater agreement and precision in our application of words than we otherwise could. No words for primary modalities of sense, such as 'green', 'soft', 'sweet', 'middle C', can be rendered precise by analysis or by synonyms; but by synthetic definitions we have correlated some of them with matters that can be measured very precisely and very consistently.

The great disadvantage of a synthetic definition is that it may be mistaken for an analytic one. That it would be analytic method to define 'triangle' as meaning a threesided straightsided closed figure, and synthetic method to define it as meaning the first closed figure discussed in Euclid's *Elements*, is obvious. It is also obvious that the definition of '21' as meaning the successor of 20 is analytic, while the definition of it as meaning the smallest positive integer that cannot be named by a single English word standing alone is synthetic.

But in many cases the distinction is not so obvious. For

example, many persons insist that colour *is* a certain wave-length; many others insist, in effect, that this is the error of taking a synthetic definition for an analytic one. For another example, of which sort is G. E. Moore's definition of 'beauty' as 'that of which the admiring contemplation is good'? If it is an analytic definition it means: 'In calling a thing beautiful I mean only that it is good to contemplate that thing admiringly.' If it is synthetic it means: ' "Beauty" is the name I give to some quality which I shall not analyse; but you will know which quality I mean when I say that it is the only quality which it is always good to contemplate admiringly.'

The main subject of *Principia Ethica*, from which comes this definition of 'beauty', is the definition or indefinability of good. Though this question is expressly distinguished by the author from the question of the nominal definition of the word 'good', it may nevertheless be correctly represented as the question whether such propositions as 'The good is that which satisfies', when taken as definitions of the word 'good', are definitions by analysis or by synthesis.

It is thus often difficult to tell whether a definition is proceeding analytically or synthetically, and easy to mistake a synthetic definition for an analytic one. Now this leads to error. If there is some red other than wavelengths, so that the definition of 'red' by wavelengths is synthetic, those who take it for analytic are overlooking a certain most important reality. Those who think that synthetic definitions are being mistaken for analytic appeal to Butler's dictum that 'everything is what it is, and not another thing'. To them the insistence of Ogden and Richards on the synthetic method seems like saying that no word has any meaning of its own, but every word means what is meant by some combination of other words. In an analytic definition there is a definiens expression which means the same as the definiend word (except for 'the paradox of analysis', discussed below, pp. 171–89); but in a synthetic definition there is not. The quality which 'red' means is the quality correlated with wavelength (say) 6,500 to 7,000 Angstroms; but 'red' does not mean what is meant by 'the quality correlated with wavelength 6,500–7,000 Angstroms'.

An obvious case of the error insinuated by synthetic

definitions is the genetic fallacy, for example, that every man is the child he used to be rather than the man he is now, or that if some of our remote ancestors were not monogamous it is unnatural and wrong for us to be monogamous.

Let us suppose that this sort of error is always avoided, and that a synthetic definition is always fully recognized as such. A further disadvantage of this method remains, which may be introduced by asking: does such a definition really achieve its purpose of making a man know what the word means, or does it merely tell him that the word means that x, whatever it may be, which fulfils certain conditions?

The synthetic definition of 'triangle' as meaning the first closed figure discussed in Euclid's *Elements* will not teach me the important fact that a triangle has three sides unless I look in the book. On the other hand, the synthetic definition of a point by reference to co-ordinates seems to give me the point; and the synthetic definition of 'i' as the square root of minus one seems to give the whole meaning of 'i'.

The answer seems to be that synthetic definition does not give me the meaning of the word unless either the word means something logically determined by the relation given or I am otherwise acquainted with the thing meant. The synthetic definition of 'i' gives me the meaning because the whole nature of i is logically necessitated by the relation given in the definition. The synthetic definition of 'triangle' by reference to Euclid's book does not by itself do this because there is no logically necessary connexion between being a triangle and being the first plane figure discussed in a book. I must in addition be acquainted with the figure triangle and with its position in the *Elements*.

We distinguished in a previous section that sort of word-thing definition which acquaints a man with a new sort of thing because what the word means is something new to him. We now see that the synthetic method of word-thing definition cannot do this except when the thing meant belongs to the realm of pure logic and the definition approaches it through purely logical relations. Otherwise the thing meant must be already known to the learner if a synthetic definition of the name for it is to succeed. Out-side of logic and mathematics, therefore, synthetic definition does not make a man acquainted with a new thing at the same time as it acquaints him with a new usage. Otherwise the synthetic definition of colour-words would make the blind see.

This defect in the synthetic method has caused many people to deny it the name of 'definition'. ' "*Feuillemorte*" is the colour of withered leaves falling in autumn.' Locke does not wish to call this a 'definition' (III xi. 14). Yet it conforms perfectly to his definition of 'definition' as 'showing the meaning of one word by several other not synonymous terms' (III iv. 6). This reveals that Locke mistook his own usage of the word 'definition'. He really used it in a narrower sense than he supposed, somewhat as follows: 'Definition is showing the meaning of one word by several other not synonymous terms, where the hearer becomes acquainted for the first time through these other terms with the thing meant by the word being defined.' It is because these words will not acquaint a man with the colour feuillemorte that Locke denies them to be a definition, although they will tell one who is acquainted with this colour that the word 'feuillemorte' means it. So Locke's conception of definition is not so purely nominal as he supposes; it still secretly includes the idea of getting new knowledge about *things*. A definition is not a definition, to him, unless it can not merely give a man the knowledge that this word means this thing, but also give him the knowledge of this thing for the first time. Many other persons, including many who like Locke regard definition as always nominal, have thus limited their notion of definition to sentences that can give a man the thing as well as the word for the first time.

We owe the clear and emphatic introduction of the synthetic method to W. E. Johnson.[1] He remarks that all the definitions occurring in a symbolic system, whether logical or mathematical, should in his view be synthetic and never analytic.

A view apparently equivalent to the view that mathematical definitions always *are* synthetic was stated by Bertrand Russell in 1902: 'Mathematical definition consists in pointing out a fixed relation to a fixed term, of which one

[1] *Logic*, I 108–9.

term only is capable: this term is then defined by means of the fixed relation and the fixed term.'[1]

Professor C. I. Lewis gives an interesting and somewhat different account of the synthetic method under the name of 'definition by description'. The definition of sounds in terms of harmonic motion, he writes, represents a type of definition quite common in science, and is of a peculiar sort which may be called 'definition by description'. It proceeds by referring to some character of the thing that is non-essential but uniformly present in all known cases of it and absent in all other known cases. A traditional example would be: 'Man is the animal that laughs.'

'It is a distinguishing feature of such definition by description', he writes, 'that the relation of definiens to definiendum which it states is one requiring to be established by induction and incapable of being established by logical analysis alone. Correlatively, the criterion of the definiendum which such a definition specifies is one (supposedly) sufficient for selecting what the definiendum denotes in all actual circumstances, but *not* sufficient to select what is defined under all thinkable circumstances or from among all imaginable things. The behavioristic or the brain-state theory of mind involves such definition of the mental by description.'[2]

Professor Lewis's 'definition by description' includes elements of my analytic method as well as my synthetic method. He seems to be referring to the analytic method when he gives 'man is the animal that laughs' as an example, and when he regards the process as consisting in referring to some *property* of the thing meant by the word being defined. (He does not use the word 'property'; but he indicates nearly what the inventor of that term meant by it when he says it is a characteristic that is non-essential but uniformly present in all known cases of it and absent from all other known cases.) So far, then, he regards 'definition by description' as not going outside the thing meant by the word, whereas the term 'synthetic definition' implies that we do go outside the thing: instead of giving a property of the thing we relate it to another thing. On the other hand, all of Professor Lewis's other examples of his 'definition by description' seem to be

---

[1] *The Principles of Mathematics*, I 27.
[2] *Journal of Philosophy*, 1941, p. 231.

definitions by a relation rather than by a property. Thus he refers to the definition of sounds by means of their relation to harmonic motion, and of mental things by means of their relation to the brain.

I wish to disregard those parts of Professor Lewis's account which suggest the analytic method, and make a remark about those which suggest the synthetic method. Replacing, therefore, his term 'character' by the term 'relation', I observe that he explicitly confines his 'definition by description' to cases where the relation is ascertained by *induction*. It is by induction that we learn that sounds are connected with vibrations, and thoughts with the brain. My 'synthetic method', on the contrary, covers all cases where the thing meant is indicated by referring to a relation it bears to other things, whether our knowledge of this relation is inductive or deductive. The difference between the case where the relation is induced and that where it is logically necessary is certainly very important. We have seen that only in the latter can synthetic definition give the meaning of a word without the aid of prior acquaintance with the thing. And the value of Professor Lewis's emphasis on the inductive element in 'definition by description' is illustrated by the *Oxford English Dictionary*'s synthetic definition of 'gold' as 'the most precious metal', since gold has recently ceased to be the most precious metal.

The defect of synthetic definition in inductive matters has been insisted on by Professor E. W. Hall in a way that may be condensed as follows:

'By "the fallacy of correlational definition" I mean definition of a term by a correlate, with the consequent obliteration of an intensional difference. E.g., a correlational definition of 'blue' would be: the retinal stimulation of a normal organism by light waves between 4250 A and 4750 A. ⟨It is weak because⟩

'(1) A one-one correlation can be established only if the terms have intensional difference. Thus the attempt to eliminate one of these intensions by reducing it to the other is selfcontradictory.

'(2) It is restricted to terms whose extensions are denumerable classes, because only such can be put in one-one correspondence. In any case the one-one correlation has not been established, but taken by an "inductive leap", which is disguised.

'(3) The intuitive factor in knowledge cannot be eliminated by correlational techniques and definitions. It is impossible to determine the extensional correlates of properties unless one be acquainted with the properties *per se*.'[1]

This is rather more unfavourable to the synthetic method than the case warrants. In the first place, Professor Hall ignores the fact that other methods of definition may be impossible for a given word or in given circumstances. In the second place, the correlational definition of blue which he suggests has considerable use: it provides a way of making our applications of the term 'blue' much more precise and consistent; it enables us all to agree much more closely where blue changes into green. As a means of strictly nominal definition, whether through purely logical connexions or through inductive connexions to some experienced property, the synthetic method is certainly of use. And the connexion of blue with a certain wavelength, though involving an inductive leap, is extremely well established.

But the error which Professor Hall has in mind is that such synthetic definitions may be taken for analytic, taken, that is, to lead us to the thing signified by giving us an analysis of that thing. He fears that the truth that the quality meant by the word 'blue' *is correlated with* a certain wavelength may be carelessly stated and become the falsehood that the quality blue *is* a certain wavelength.

§ 4. **The Implicative Method.** Fourthly, consider the sentence, 'A square has two diagonals, and each of them divides the square into two rightangled isosceles triangles'. It does not profess to be about words at all. It is not explicitly a nominal definition; for it does not say that 'the word means so and so'. Yet a person who comes to it knowing the meaning of all the words in it except 'diagonal' can learn from it what the word 'diagonal' means. And therefore a person who wants to define the word 'diagonal', in the sense of teaching some other person what it means, can do so by uttering this sentence.

The method here exemplified of giving a nominal definition differs in two important respects from all of the methods previously described.

[1] *Psychological Review*, 1942, pp. 162–5.

1. It uses the word being defined and does not mention it, whereas the previous methods mention the word being defined and do not use it. To use a word is to refer to the thing the word means by the method of uttering the word; but to mention a word is to utter it, in inverted commas, not for the ordinary purpose of referring to what it ordinarily means, but for the unusual purpose of referring to itself. To say, ' "Life" is a short word', is to mention the word 'life'. But to say, 'Life is short', is to use it. He who mentions a word is referring to the word; but he who uses a word is referring to what the word means.

2. All the previous methods provide a phrase equivalent to the word being defined. If we define 'automobile' by synonym as a motor-car, 'motor-car' is a phrase equivalent to the phrase 'automobile'. If we define it by analysis as a mechanically selfpropelled roadvehicle, 'mechanically selfpropelled roadvehicle' is an equivalent phrase. If we define it by synthesis as the kind of vehicle most common on the roads of Canada in 1935, there again is an equivalent phrase. But the definition above provides no phrase equivalent to the word 'diagonal'. Here for the first time we come to a method of definition that does not depend on equivalence.

As to names, we may call it the 'implicative' method, because it provides a sentence which implies that the word means so and so. We might also call it the 'contextual' method, because it puts the word in a context which determines its sense. Gergonne, who probably was the first to describe it, called it 'implicit' definition in his excellent article on definition.

The implicative method is closely connected with the synthetic method. Probably most implicative definitions can be transformed into synthetic definitions; if so, though they do not give an equivalence in their implicative form, they imply one. When mathematicians say that a system dispenses with definitions because the terms are defined by the postulates in which they occur, the postulates are implicative definitions of the terms. It is not clear to what extent implicative definitions are possible outside mathematics, nor to what extent we actually use this method. An implicative definition might define different terms for different people, depending on which of those in the sentence they already knew.

§ 5. **The Denotative Method.** We sometimes hear it said that: 'Definition is a useless procedure. The meaning of words is always actually learned by examples. We do not tell a child that "bird" means feathered vertebrate. We say it means such things as swans and robins and geese and hens and larks, and not such things as bats or butterflies or aeroplanes.'

In this statement the word 'definition' is used in a narrower sense than mine. In my sense teaching the meaning of a word by examples is one method of word-thing definition, for by 'word-thing definition' I mean all teaching the meaning of a word. Translated into my language, the above statement is that the use of examples is the only good method of word-thing definition. All other methods are bad. And people who make this statement usually have in mind mainly the analytical method as that which they are contrasting with the use of examples.

There is undoubtedly a method of word-thing definition, quite distinct from any we have yet described, which consists in mentioning examples of what the word applies to. These examples may be either particular things to which the word applies, or sorts of thing to which it applies. To explain 'bird' as meaning swans and robins and so on is to mention sorts of bird, not particular birds. On the other hand, we explain the word 'ocean' by mentioning particular things to which it applies, if we say: 'The word "ocean" means the Atlantic and the Pacific and things like them.' Carnap in his *Introduction to Semantics*, pp. 57–8, defines the phrases 'descriptive sign' and 'logical sign' by giving long lists of particular signs to which these names are to apply.

One obvious name for this method is the 'exemplifying' or 'exemplificatory' method or 'exemplification'. But I shall usually call it the 'denotative' method, in order to have the benefit of the well known doctrine of denotation and connotation. The word 'ocean' *denotes* the Atlantic and the Pacific and only two or three other things, because there are only these few things that have the connotation which the word 'ocean' *connotes*, namely, a huge body of water not enclosed by land. Thus by the 'denotation' of a given word I usually mean roughly either all the particular things to which it is applied or all the classes which include all and only the particular things to which it is applied. And by the 'connotation' of a word I usually mean roughly the common characteristic or sort or class in virtue of which the word is applied to these and only these things. Thus the word 'man' connotes a certain complex property, and can be used as part of a descriptive phrase to denote anything that has this property.

I do not wish to define precisely how I am going to use the words 'connotation' and 'denotation', or to confine myself to a single rigid usage; but it is desirable to point out one common sense which I shall never use. The word 'fox' denotes all the animals which have a certain character, a specific form of mammalianness, and it connotes this character. But the word 'fox' also suggests something quite different from this specific form of mammalianness, namely, cunning. 'Fox' does not mean cunning, and its denotation is not everything that is cunning. Yet the suggestion of cunning has got itself firmly attached to the word as a kind of secondary flavour or association, a kind of improper but regularized meaning in addition to the proper one. Such a secondary flavour or association of a word is often called by grammarians the 'connotation' of the word. And that is a sense which I shall never use. My sense, or something close to it, is the common one in books on logic.

The denotative method of word-thing definition, then, consists in mentioning some part of the denotation of the word, some one or more of the things to which the word is applied. (It is usually impossible to recite the whole of the denotation. We do not have names for all birds or for all sorts of bird. We could not possibly name the birds that have not yet hatched; but they are included in the denotation of 'bird'.) We hope that from this hint the hearer will learn what the word means and how to apply it.

Does he learn it? Is the denotative method successful? Or, rather, to what extent does he learn it and under what conditions? For of course it must be successful sometimes.

Contrary opinions are held about the utility of the denotative method. Some persons come near to declaring that it is the only effective method of word-thing definition; though, as we have seen, they usually express this, in language different from mine, by saying that 'definition is a useless procedure, and the meaning of words is always actually learned from examples'. Professor Dubs declared in the *Philosophical Review* for 1943 that completely exact denotative definitions are possible for all ultimates that may need to be defined. He did not undertake to prove the point in that place, however, except to remark that 'the three requirements for giving denotative definitions are obviously obtainable in most cases at least'. The three requirements which he had in mind were '(*a*) a clear and exact notion of the meaning of a term on the part of one person, (*b*) situations that contain varied examples of that term, and (*c*) an attentive and intelligent listener'.

Others, however, hold a low opinion of the usefulness of the denotative method, and among them is Professor C. I. Lewis: It is less conclusive, because 'no collection of cases . . is ever sufficient to determine uniquely the denotation of a term', and because the hearer may be unable to make the necessary analysis. Hence the actual use of exemplification is almost confined to 'conveying the meaning of a *word* where the *concept* itself is already something shared'.[1]

We may safely reject the extreme view that example is the only good method of word-thing definition. We have examined several other methods enough to know that they too have their use. Furthermore, there are words whose meaning could not possibly be conveyed by examples, such as 'million'. In fact, no mathematical term can be defined by examples alone with sufficient precision for mathematical use. Those who suppose that example is the only and sufficient means of word-thing definition can only be persons who tend to exclude mathematical language from their reflections on language.

On the other hand, persons whose thought is largely mathematical or logical tend to underrate the value of definition by example in other spheres. We often can effectively

[1] *Mind and the World Order*, pp. 78–9.

define 'sulk' by saying that Achilles was sulking when he
refused to fight because he had not received his due share of
the spoils. We often can effectively define 'brave' by saying
that a child is brave if he does not show distress when there
is thunder or when he goes to the dentist.

Professor Lewis objects that the hearer may be unable to
make the necessary analysis. For example, Achilles by re-
maining in his tent was resting and waiting and sheltering as
well as sulking, and the learner might pick out any one
of these and suppose it to be the meaning of 'sulk'. The
example offered is always a complex affair, having more parts
or aspects than are concerned in the present matter; and the
hearer must be able to distinguish these parts or aspects
enough to abstract the one intended. Just so the hearer of
a parable, 'The Kingdom of Heaven shall come like a thief
in the night', must be able to abstract the one character of
the Kingdom of Heaven that resembles a thief in the night
from the many that do not.

It is true that the hearer must abstract from the example
the one character in virtue of which it is an example, and
that he may not be able to do so. It is also true, as Professor
Lewis perhaps implies, that, in some cases where the hearer
cannot make the abstraction when aided only by the example
and the as yet meaningless word, he can make it when aided
only by an analytical definition and the word. Probably also
there are cases where he requires the help of both an example
and an analytical definition. It is surely false that there are
no cases where the hearer succeeds in making the abstraction
for the first time in his life by means of examples alone, and
probably false also that the addition of an analysis is of any
use at all for giving young children their first grasp of the
names of common human states like courage and envy and
love. Such things as jealousy and hate are probably all complex, and therefore probably their names can all be explained
by analytical definitions in the manner of Spinoza,[1] but only
to adults; children can learn their meaning only by hearing
the name applied to examples.

From the fact that the hearer may be unable to make the
necessary analysis, Professor Lewis infers that the actual

[1] *Ethics,* III end.

use of exemplification is almost confined to conveying the meaning of a *word* where the *concept* is already shared. Does this imply that the successful use of examples is almost confined to introducing a new name for something for which the learner already has some other name? That would be far too strong. It would still be too strong if we weakened it to imply only that the successful use of examples is almost confined to introducing a name for something which the learner has already abstracted from experience or constructed in his mind. Examples are used successfully even in cases where the learner, far from having some name for the thing already, has never before abstracted the thing from the mass of his experience. Mentioning examples and ascribing the name to them is the very means by which human beings are first brought to make hundreds of their abstractions.

Professor Lewis has another objection to the exemplificatory method, which may be developed as follows. If I do succeed in abstracting an element from the complex mentioned, how do I know it is the right one, since the example has all sorts of aspects? Hundreds of persons erroneously believe that the word 'paradoxical' means selfcontradictory. They do this because their only way of learning the meaning of the word has been from examples to which they heard it applied, and all those examples have been utterances that were selfcontradictory. They have abstracted an element that was really in all the examples offered to them, but yet is not the element actually meant by the word. For a paradox is a statement seemingly absurd, and selfcontradictions are common among the examples of it merely because a selfcontradiction is a very obvious case of the seemingly absurd.

Further examples of the paradoxical may remove this false impression that it is the selfcontradictory; and then, if the learner can make a new abstraction fitting his enlarged set of cases, he will have a better theory of what the word means. But will he necessarily be correct even now? It seems not, for it seems that at any moment he may hear some new application of the word which will not fit his theory. And this may apparently go on indefinitely, because, as Professor

Lewis says, 'no collection of cases . . is ever sufficient to determine uniquely the denotation of a term'.

It seems then that what is achieved by the method of
examples is never better than an *hypothesis* about the meaning
of a word. The hypothesis can be verified to the extent of
being known to fit all applications of the word yet known to
me; but it always remains possible that to-morrow some
person who knows English better than I do will apply the
word so as to show me that my theory of its meaning is
wrong. As James Mackaye[1] put it, the derivation of connotative understanding from denotative is a special case of
the verification of hypotheses. Though general agreement
is no test of truth in general, general agreement in the use
of a word *is* a test of a hypothesis about the meaning of
that word. What Socrates really has to verify is whether
Euthyphro's account of the connotation of 'piety' fits our
actual applications of the word.

The main thing to say about this objection to the exemplificatory method is that it points to a real defect, but a defect
of language in general rather than of an optional method of
definition. The vast majority of the words used by any
person must always remain in a hypothetical condition. Only
within a narrow specified language like a mathematical
system, if anywhere at all, can the meaning of all the words
be certainly the same to all who would ordinarily be said to
understand the language. The domain of mathematics at
any time is the domain which down to that time men have
succeeded in covering with perfectly precise and perfectly
public terms. It is being extended and will be enormously
larger than it is now, but there will always be a vast area
outside it.

A more specific rebuttal of this objection to the exemplifying method is that the meaning of some words is primarily
denotative and only secondarily connotative, and for them
examples are the best method of definition. In these words
the denotation determines the connotation rather than, what
logicians often declare, the connotation determines the denotation. That the word is applied to these particulars is a
more central and abiding element in its usage than that it

[1] *The Logic of Language*, pp. 83–5.

connotes a certain character. What is romanticism (in the literary context)? It is Shelley, Wordsworth, Keats, Scott, in contrast with Austen, Dryden, Pope. Such examples as these are the most permanent and widespread element in the meaning of the word 'romanticism'. They remain, while each writer's attempt to reach the connotation is discarded in turn. No one would ever think of assigning to the word a connotation such that Pope was a romantic and Keats was not.

All effective definitions of the literary sense of 'romantic' are denotative. There is no synonym for it. There is no agreed analysis of it. It cannot be defined synthetically because we do not know clearly just what it involves. And many other words are such; that is to say, what they mean is primarily certain cases. There is a feeling that these are the cases of some one general connotation; but it remains obscure what that connotation is, and in any conflict between the examples and a suggested connotation the examples will win. In most of us, as Mackaye put it, denotative understanding is better developed than connotative.

There is another class of words, for which it is very desirable to have both a denotative and a connotative definition. These are the strange and frequent words whose denotation and connotation are in conflict. If in practice men refuse to apply a word to some of the cases that possess what they connote by the word, a conscientious account of actual usage will state both what men connote by the word and what things they apply it to.

But is there such a class of words? Two distinct parties tell us that there is not, the logicians and the behaviourists. The logicians regularly say that the connotation of a word *determines* its denotation, and the denotation depends entirely on the connotation, so that there could not possibly be a clash between the two. A behaviourist, on the other hand, may maintain that denotative meaning is the only kind of meaning, so that according to him too there cannot be a conflict.

To the behaviourist the reply is that people certainly offer, in the case of many of their words, analytical accounts of the connotation which are verbally quite distinct from any list

of the denotates of the word. And when I say that the connotation of some words conflicts with their denotation, this
may be taken to mean, if preferred, that the analytical
accounts which their users give of the meanings of these
words do not fit the cases to which they apply them.

To the logicians the reply is that their doctrine that connotation determines denotation is at best a true account of the
ideal or *rational* relation between the connotation and the
denotation of a word. It is certainly not a true account of
their *actual* relation in every case. The logicians have failed
to make it clear that they are describing an ideal of reason,
and not actual human speech. The rational thing is perhaps
always to establish a certain connotation for a word and then
apply it only to things that have that connotation. But we
are not always rational. And this is not merely that each of
us makes errors of identification, and sometimes takes a rook
for a crow. There are words which whole groups of us
regularly apply in conflict with what we connote by them.

You will naturally ask me to give you examples of such
words, and I must try to do so. But first I ask you to agree
that there is a peculiar difficulty about giving examples in
this case. To apply a word to a set of things which is not the
set indicated by one's connotation for the word, is irrational.
No one wishes to be irrational. No one, therefore, wishes to
admit that he himself uses words so that their denotation
and connotation conflict. No example, therefore, that could
be offered would be convincing to everyone. The best I can
hope is that at least one of my examples will be convincing
to every reader.

William Empson argues that those who use the term
'proletarian art' decline to apply it to all the cases to which,
on their account of its connotation, they ought to apply it.
The term, he says, is liable to a 'false limitation'.[1] 'It is not
obvious why [W. W. Jacobs] is not a proletarian author, and
it would annoy a communist very much to admit that he was.'
The reason for the discrepancy is in this case connected with
the loyalties and other emotions aroused by the term.

Is it not true that we white English-speakers mean by
'a native' of a country a person born and bred in the country,

[1] *Some Versions of Pastoral*, pp. 3, 7.

and yet shrink from applying the word to many persons who exhibit this connotation? For instance, we decline to call a Eurasian or a white person born and bred in India a 'native' of India.

Persons who use the word 'realistic' as a term of art-criticism usually say, if asked to give its connotation, that it means depicting people and things as they really are, instead of fantastically or ideally. Yet there is one sort of representation of people as they really are, to which these speakers never apply the word 'realistic', namely, the representation of good and pleasant people as they really are.

The term 'propaganda' seems to be limited in the same false way. Its emotional reverberations make people decline to apply it to some of the cases to which it does apply by their account of its connotation. Senator Taft obtained the passage of an amendment to the Soldiers' Voting Law of 1944, by which amendment it became unlawful in the United States for any officer or executive to deliver to the troops 'any motion picture film, or other literature or material . . . containing political argument or political propaganda of any kind designed or calculated to affect the result of any election for President'. When the authorities on the ground of this amendment withheld from the troops a new biography of Justice Holmes and a film about Woodrow Wilson, Senator Taft was indignant and complained that he had been misunderstood. Yet probably the connotation of the word 'propaganda', both to him and to the army's officers, *was* such as to make a film about Woodrow Wilson propaganda for presidential elections.

A very mild case of this sort of error probably exists in most of our minds about the word 'money'. Probably most of us have a tendency to classify cheques as money, and yet we connote by 'money' generalized purchasing power capable of being transferred from person to person indefinitely many times.[1]

This discrepancy between connotation and denotation is one of the reasons why dictionaries often explain a word by first giving a connotative definition and then saying 'applied especially to', or sometimes just 'applied to'.

[1] G. D. H. Cole, *Money: Its Present and Future* (1944), p. 28.

There are, then, many cases where the denotative method of definition is desirable, and many where it is necessary.

The world of symbolic logic is very far from the concrete world where the denotative method is most at home; but there is a faint resemblance to the denotative method in the 'matrix definition' of symbolic logic. It is a matrix definition to say: By 'p implies q' I mean that either p and q are both true or they are both false or p is false and q is true. The one case excluded is p true and q false. The definition proceeds by making an exhaustive list of possibilities and saying of each whether it is to be denoted by 'implication'. The word 'implication', so defined, either has no connotation or at least its connotation is irrelevant to everything said about it in the system that defines it by a matrix.

Professor G. E. Moore and thinkers whom he has influenced often indicate a meaning by saying, 'I mean that sense of the word in which we say that . . .', and then giving a sentence using the word unmistakably in the required sense. In this way Professor Malcolm, for example, points out a particular meaning of the word 'certain' in *Mind* for 1942. This procedure may recall to our minds the denotative method of definition, because it relies on an example to indicate a meaning. However, it is not precisely definition at all, in my sense of reporting or establishing a meaning. It is a method of reminding us of a meaning we already know and use, and of separating it from other meanings of the word. It would not work if we did not already know and use the word in that meaning.

§ 6. **The Ostensive Method.** The five methods so far described—the synonymous, the analytic, the synthetic, the implicative, and the denotative—all define a word by using other words. They all assume that the learner already knows the meaning of some words. And they are all quite useless to a baby who knows no words at all.

There must therefore be at least one more method of defining a word, and it must be a method that can dispense with words altogether (except the word being defined).

How then do we go about the enterprise of teaching the meaning of a word without using other words? Here we must distinguish two very different cases. Either the learner already has the general idea of symbolization, and needs only to learn that this form is a symbol and symbolizes that thing, or he has not yet acquired the general idea of symbolization and has to do so in learning that this word is a symbol of that thing. The latter has to be done only once in a lifetime, and is immensely more difficult.

We have a unique autobiographical record of a person achieving the idea of symbolization for the first time: Helen Keller's account of the sudden flash in which it came to her that a human act could symbolize something and that her nurse was symbolizing in moving her finger-tip on Helen's palm. In this case the discovery was delayed beyond the usual time by the lack of sight and hearing, and probably also by the indistinct form of letters drawn on the palm with a finger-tip, and therefore came as a sudden wonderful revelation. Miss Keller does not record that she had herself copied these motions before she realized that they were symbols. The ordinary child hears strikingly individual sounds, and produces them himself many times, and gradually associates them with objects, and so grows slowly into the realization that the sound symbolizes the object it is associated with. Before this realization has arrived, he needs to have the sound repeated many times in the presence of the object if he is to associate them and eventually to realize that one is a symbol of the other, and can be used to refer to the other in its absence. After the general realization, repetition is necessary only to help him to memorize and to correct errors of application; it is no longer necessary to convey the idea that he is in the presence of a symbol.

6.1. The method of that first great definition, the conveyance of the idea of symbolization itself, is then only to keep on symbolizing, to keep on naming present objects and encouraging the child to do so, taking care to make the forms both of the objects and of their names as sharp as possible.

6.2. When this has been achieved, it is sometimes possible to define new words simply by uttering them when their objects are engrossing the attention of the learner.

6.3. More often, however, it is necessary not merely to utter the word in the presence of the object but at the same time to point to the object. Most objects whose names have to be learnt do not engross the attention beyond possibility of mistake, especially if they are not collections of matter with an obvious shape and colour moving as wholes. Pointing is itself a symbol whose meaning has to be taught, and it is taught early because it immensely facilitates later definitions.

6.4. A special form of pointing is the demonstrative word, such as 'this', 'here', 'now', 'to-day', 'she', whose meaning at each utterance is determined in part by the time or place or author of the utterance. These words are often used along with pointing to the present object. A man may say 'that is a dahlia' and point as he does so, to explain what 'dahlia' means.

6.5. Demonstrative words are also used without gestures and in the absence of the object meant by the word being defined. 'Redfigure vases are the sort you saw yesterday in my study.' This definition of 'redfigure' proceeds in the absence of the object, and uses three demonstratives; 'you', 'yesterday', 'my'.

6.6. If the word means a form distinguishable by the eyes, its meaning can be given by drawings. Accordingly, Locke thought it 'not unreasonable to propose, that [in a dictionary] words standing for things which are known and distinguished by their outward shapes, should be expressed by little draughts and prints made of them' (III xi. 25). For suitable words, such pictures can do more to explain the meaning than even an analytic definition, although an analytic definition may be possible. Many anatomical words can be defined analytically but are better defined by a picture. This would even be the best way to define 'man' if, as Locke the physician thinks probable, what we really mean by that word is an organism of a certain shape. But this method is impossible for words that do not mean anything to do with spatial form, and also for some that do, such as 'chiliagon'.

These six sub-methods are six different forms of what I am calling the 'ostensive' method of word-thing definition. (By 'ostensive' method I mean any method which does not rely on words alone, but also more or less directly uses the learner's experience of examples.) They differ from each other according as they:

(6.1, 6.2) use no symbol at all;

(6.3) use no symbol except the gesture of pointing;

(6.4) use words together with present objects;
(6.5) use words and not pointing or present objects;
(6.6) use drawings.

One or more of these six sub-methods were in the mind of W. E. Johnson when he introduced the notion of (6) *ostensive definition*, his second important contribution to the theory of the method of definition. (His first was the synthetic method.) He probably had most prominently in mind 6.4, such acts as defining 'dahlia' by pointing to a dahlia and saying 'that is a dahlia'; for he describes ostensive definition in one place as 'imposing a name in the act of indicating, presenting or introducing the object to which the name is to apply' (I 94). Sometimes, probably, he included 6.5, the least ostensive kind of ostensive definition; for he apparently thought it ostensive to define 'Mr. Smith' as 'the man to whom you were introduced yesterday' (I 84, top). He tended, at least on page 94, to regard the following characteristics of a word as always going together:

(1) being a proper name, that is, meaning a particular, not a general, object;
(2) not being definable by the analytic method;
(3) being definable only ostensively.

In fact, however, neither the first nor the second involves the third; and the assumption that the second involves the third contradicts his own insight into the possibility of synthetic definition. Such ambiguities or vacillations are inevitable in the first appearance of a new doctrine of importance.

Bertrand Russell was thinking of 6.1 or 6.2 when he wrote that 'an ostensive definition consists of a series of percepts which generate a habit'.[1] The book from which this comes is mainly about ostensive definition in this sense.

There is a resemblance and also a difference between what I call the 'ostensive' and what I call the 'denotative' methods of word-thing definition. The resemblance is that they both achieve the end by referring the learner to examples of the thing meant (or, in the case of a proper name, by referring him to the thing itself). The difference is that the denotative

---

[1] *Inquiry into Meaning and Truth*, p. 157.

method uses only words, and only non-demonstrative words, while the ostensive method uses demonstrative words and the presence of the examples to perception. If one tried to make a man know what the word 'pleasantness' meant by producing a rose and letting him smell it, and then producing chocolate and letting him taste it, and so on, that would be ostensive method. But if, without producing any rose or chocolate, one merely told him that pleasantness is a characteristic common to the experiences of smelling roses and tasting chocolate, and so on, that would be denotative method. Professor Broad, however, from whom I have taken this example, once called the latter 'ostensive definition', thus destroying all necessary connexion of the term 'ostensive' with some perception present at the time of uttering the definition, which I think a pity, and contrary to the intention of W. E. Johnson.[1]

The essential insight, which Johnson's theory of ostensive definition expressed, was that, since our words are related to and signify our perceptual experience, and must do so if language is to be of any use to us and our human purposes are to be achieved, no account of the process of learning words can be complete without discussing how words get related to perceptible things, and that no previous account of definition had sufficiently brought out this process of establishing the connexion between language and things. All previous accounts had, like the first five methods of definition described here, regarded the definition of words as proceeding always by means of words already understood. Pascal, for example, had told us to define all obscure or uncertain words by means of those words whose meaning God has implanted in us so clearly as to be beyond all doubt, and to refrain from trying to define the latter.

But God has not implanted in us the meaning of any word at all. If, therefore, the meaning of all words were given only through other words, the meaning of all words would be circular. Words would have meaning only in the way in which a square on a chessboard has meaning. Each square is in a definite and unique relation to the rest, and we can get from one to any other in certain definite ways; but no

[1] C. D. Broad, *Five Types of Ethical Theory*, pp. 186–7.

square means anything outside the chessboard. But words are evidently significant in another dimension beside that in which the chessboard square is significant. The word 'pipit' has relations to the word 'bird' and the word 'reptile' and the word 'vertebrate' and so on, and these are faintly like the relations of the squares to each other; but in addition the word 'pipit' has relations to things visible, audible, and tangible, that are not symbols at all, namely, the pipits.

Instead of Pascal's tendency to believe that the connexion between words and things is in some cases implanted in us by God, we have nowadays a tendency to belittle the importance of this connexion or even deny its existence. Thus, Professor Lewis wrote that 'all definition is . . circular ⟨and⟩ the difference between a good and a bad ⟨one⟩ is only . . . the diameter of the circle'.[1] 'All the terms in the dictionary, however ideal its definitions, will be themselves defined'; and 'the conceptual meaning of a term is nothing whatever apart from other such meanings'. He admits that community of meaning may be verified by 'exhibiting the denotation' as well as by 'definition'. But he holds the former 'less conclusive' and 'confined almost exclusively to conveying the meaning of a *word* where the *concept* itself is already something shared'. These views seem to imply that swans and our traffic with them have little or nothing to do with our coming to mean the same by the word 'swan'.

Professor Carnap asserted a more extreme form of this view when he wrote that so called 'ostensive' definitions are translations of words; to define 'elephant' ostensively is merely to lay down the transformation-rule: '"elephant" = animal of the same kind as the animal in this or that position in space-time'.[2]

Professor Ayer[3] concedes all that can truly be conceded to this view when he writes that ostensive definition is not logically indispensable to communication; 'for it is logically conceivable that people should use words correctly and understand their meaning without any process of learning at all'. 'We have, however', he writes, 'good reason to suppose

---

[1] *Mind and the World Order*, p. 82.
[2] *The Unity of Science*, tr. Max Black, p. 39.
[3] *The Foundations of Empirical Knowledge*, 1947, p. 94.

that the correct use of symbols has, in fact, to be learned.' We have indeed; and the tendency to belittle ostensive definition or change its nature is an aberration of those who are bewitched by the fairyland of symbolic systems detached from experience.

> The beldame sans meaning
> Thee hath in thrall.

A truer view of the matter is put by Professor Grace Delaguna.[1] 'Only through the *convergence of action* upon the objects of verbal response', she writes, does 'language become standardized, and its terms freed from ambiguity and vagueness'. Where language has been highly developed, it is possible to establish or correct the meaning of terms without resort to primary behaviour. I may discover from the verbal context of a new term what its meaning is, and we may agree upon definitions (i.e. analytic or synthetic definitions). But that is possible only because we already possess a multitude of words standardized through practical co-operation.

How sure is the ostensive method? Is it more or less likely to achieve the desired result than other methods? Miss Wodehouse has suggested an answer to this question.[2] W. E. Johnson, she says, implied that pointing with the finger is superior to verbal indicating; but that is an error, which he has made plausible by describing it in language that assumed it to be successful. That it is not always successful, however, Miss Wodehouse infers from the many times Helen Keller's nurse had to write in her hand before Helen understood.

The example of Helen Keller applies only to that first ostensive definition by which we get the idea of symbolism itself (6.1). It is very true that this original definition is a laborious affair, and one cannot say beforehand just when it will be achieved. On the other hand, the ostensive method is the only method available for this purpose; all others are useless here. And the purpose *is* achieved with most human beings in the end. And when it is not achieved we call the person an idiot and believe that his brain is very different from the normal. Once the idea of symbolism has been

---

[1] *Speech, Its Function and Development*, New Haven, 1927, pp. 272–3.
[2] *Mind*, 1939, p. 233.

achieved, is ostensive method without any words (6.2 and 6.3) more, or less, sure than pointing accompanied by words (6.4)? Undoubtedly less sure. If the learner knows any words that can be used to help the definition, such as 'this', the use of them will make success more probable. In general, since none of the methods is necessarily successful in any particular instance, we always increase the likelihood that we have conveyed the meaning of the word if we use more than one of them. The peculiar advantages of definition by pointing are only two. First, it is available before any other method is, namely, at the beginning of each symbolizer's life. Second, it aims more directly than any other method at what is the primary function of very many of our words, to be names of the forms that we recognize as recurring in our experience. 'Blue', 'dog', 'house'; these words are appointed primarily to remind us of certain forms or qualities which we recognize as presented to us again and again in the course of our lives. Since the chief job of these words is to refer us to a recognizable recurring character or pattern in the world we live in, there is much to be said for the method of defining them by presenting them along with examples of their meaning.

The peculiar disadvantage of ostensive definition is that its level of precision is low for general words. We are always confronted with so much, that the likelihood of our all picking out precisely the same elements from the example as the meaning of the word being defined is very small. To achieve a useful degree of precision, the process must be repeated in several different circumstances, and somebody must be at hand to correct wrong uses of the word, which are certain to occur. No one could learn to apply the word 'dog' correctly from one ostensive definition of it. A single confrontation with the meaning of 'daw' would probably cause a person to apply the word also to starlings, ravens, crows, and rooks. Purely ostensive definitions of colour-names can reach high precision only by means of an elaborate and expensive colour-chart. This difficulty does not apply, however, to the ostensive definition of proper names.

Where both ostensive and analytic definitions of a word are possible, the analytic can usually be made much more precise. 'Square', 'cube', 'circle', are such words. Where both ostensive and synthetic definitions are possible, as of the colour-words, the synthetic can be much more precise.

This seems to raise a problem. If the learning of language must start with ostensive definitions, and other sorts of definition can occur only on the basis of previous ostensive definitions, it seems that no other sort of definition should be able to achieve a degree of precision greater than the ostensive. Every definition of whatever sort must carry with it, one would think, the vagueness of its starting-point. Yet it is obvious that this is not so. There are analytical and synthetical definitions of general characteristics that are more precise than any ostensive definitions of general characteristics. It seems that we use vaguely defined words to achieve a precise definition of some word. How do we do this? I am not prepared to answer, but it appears to be an important problem.

Not every word can be defined ostensively, for many words do not mean any form or quality that appears in experience distinct from all others. 'Nineteen', 'or', 'me', are words whose meaning cannot be learnt 'by confrontation with objects which are what they mean, or instances of what they mean'.[1] Not every word whose meaning is a particular object can be defined ostensively—for example, 'God', 'Socrates'.

Ought we to add to the words that cannot be defined by confrontation those that mean something that never occurs, such as 'phlogiston'? It seems at first thought that such words cannot possibly be learnt by meeting examples of their objects. But if the hearer *thought* he was in the presence of the object, if he had a hallucination, for example, he could be told that this object was the meaning of a certain word, and thus apparently learn by the ostensive method the meaning of a word whose object did not exist. We do seem to learn by confrontation the meaning of expressions whose objects afterwards turn out, on critical investigation, hardly to exist in the way in which we thought we collected them from experience. Thus, nearly every person learns the meaning of 'down' ostensively; and it afterwards turns out that

[1] Bertrand Russell, *Inquiry into Meaning and Truth*, p. 28.

there is no down such as he learnt, namely, no set of absolute directions inherent in space. Similarly there is no length in the absolute sense in which we seem to collect it by the ostensive definition of 'long'. The conclusion seems to be that a word's meaning something that never occurs is not an insuperable bar to its being defined ostensively.

Are there any words that can be defined *only* by confrontation with their meanings or instances of their meanings? Two classes of words have been thought to be such, namely, proper names and names of the simple, proximate qualities given in sensible experience. But we know what 'Julius Caesar' means without ever having met him; and if a man had reached maturity without hearing the word 'yellow' or any synonym for it, we could tell him that it means the colour that lies between green and orange in the spectrum. The truth is that, for language to be connected to history and sensible experience, the meaning of *some* words must be given by confrontation, but there is no particular word whose meaning must be given in this way. Some one of the names of tints must be given by confrontation; but it does not matter which, and when one has been explained by confrontation, all the others can be explained purely verbally by synthetic definitions referring to the first one. We define far more words ostensively than is necessary to cover experience with our language as fully as we do.

This does not mean that we can give a man the experience of yellow without his having normal eyes and using them. It means that we can teach him that that experience of yellow is what is meant by the word 'yellow' without requiring him to have that experience then and there. But we cannot teach him the meaning of his first colour-word, whichever it may be, without confronting him then and there with an example of its meaning; and actually we teach him all of them in that way.

§ 7. **The Rule-giving Method.** The methods so far described, and the language I have used to describe them, tend to the assumption that every word means some one thing. Of course, words may be ambiguous; but if we distinguish the various senses of an ambiguous word, and call each one of them a separate 'word', then—according to the assumption we have been implying—there is some one and only one thing that is the meaning of each word. It follows that the business of the definer of that word is to point out, by hook or by crook, the one thing that it means.

The thing in question may be either particular or general. The word 'Stalingrad' means one particular thing. The word 'sourness' means one general thing, a quality that re-appears at different times and places, but always (after ambiguities have been distinguished) the same one thing.

In other words, I have so far been writing as if every word were a name, either a proper or a general name. By a 'name' I mean here a word appointed to mean always some one and the same thing, whether a particular or a general thing. It follows that some names are not nouns. For example, not only is 'heaviness' a name in my sense, but so are 'heavy' and 'heavily' and 'heaved'.

But some words are not names. For example, the demon-strative words like 'him', 'there', 'me', 'soon', 'yesterday'. 'Yesterday' is not the name of any particular day. Nor is it the name of any special class of days. It is not a name at all. It is not a word appointed to mean always some one and the same thing. Yet it is not ambiguous. The same is true of all the demonstrative words.

Conjunctions are not names. 'And' is not the name of anything. Nor are 'not', 'nor', 'or', 'but', 'who'.

Many nouns are not names. In such a phrase as 'the Blewbers of Norfolk', 'Blewber' is not the name of any one general thing common to all the persons called 'Blewber'. If we ask 'Is she a Blewber?', we are not asking whether she exemplifies some quality. Yet the word is not ambiguous in its application to this group of people.

Nationality-words are not names. 'He is a Swiss citizen' does not mean or imply that he and all the other Swiss citizens possess, and are the sole possessors of, some general quality of which 'Swiss citizenship' is the name. Yet it is certainly a univocal word.

Cook Wilson thought that the word 'thinking' was neither the name of anything nor yet an ambiguous word. He thought that it was applied to certain forms of consciousness, to wit, (1) knowing, and (2) any other form of consciousness that depends on knowing for its occurrence, such as wondering, which is trying to get to know, and opining, which involves knowing that one does not know. 'In the case of thinking', he wrote, 'several kinds of thing are called by the same name, not because of a quality common to them but because of the manner in which they are associated in reality through the peculiar relation of one of them to the rest and the nature of their dependence upon it.'[1]

Aristotle thought that the word 'existence' was neither the name of anything nor yet an ambiguous word. He thought that it was applied (1) to substances, and (2) to anything else in so far as it belonged to a substance in its own peculiar way. Thus, to say 'there are whales and they are large' is not to use the word 'are' in two different senses; but yet 'are' is not the name of any one general thing, as 'kills' is the name of one general thing.

If there are words that are not ambiguous and yet not names, and if the six methods of word-thing definition so far described are suitable only for the definition of names, it follows that either there must be at least one more method, or some words must be left undefined. The latter alternative is absurd in our sense of 'undefined', for it would mean that there were words of which no one knew the meaning. As W. E. Johnson remarked, the problem of definition must extend to *any* word, however it may be classified by grammar. At least the problem of lexical definition must extend to all words in common use. Men want to know how to use all common words, whether or not they are names. In stipulative definition we perhaps do not have to deal with all words, because we can take over some of them from common speech without redefining them; but still we require to define many words that are not names, for examples, the conjunctions or logical operators.

What, then, is this seventh method of word-thing definition for use on words that are not names? We shall see by examining these words more closely.

Some of the above words may be called 'systematic' words. The various things to which they can properly be applied

---

[1] *Statement and Inference*, I 39; he uses the word 'name' here in another sense than mine.

are united, not by being all examples of one general quality, but by being the members of one system. The word 'existence', according to Aristotle, always refers to some member of the system of categories. The word 'thinking', according to Cook Wilson, always refers to some member of the system of forms of consciousness clustering around knowing. In 'Is she a Blewber?' the question is whether she is one of a set of humans produced by certain marriages and births; the system here is the set of those related to one male by various complications of marriage and descent in accordance with the biological laws of human reproduction and the sociological customs of the society.

Swiss citizens are the system of all the persons indicated by the complicated rules of citizenship and naturalization maintained by the Swiss Government, together with all the particular interpretations given by officials under these rules. These rules are what determines the correct application of the phrase 'Swiss citizen'. Nothing in the character of the man determines whether he is a Swiss citizen. The assertion that So-and-so is a Swiss citizen though the Government will not recognize him, to be correct, must mean that the Government is misinformed about his relations in some respect, or that it has misapplied its own rules, or that the rules ought to be changed.

In this example the notion of rules has come to the fore, and this is the key to our enlarged conception of meaning and our seventh method of word-thing definition. The essence of a univocal word, or of a univocal usage, is that it is always applied according to a single *rule*. That a word should be a name, i.e. should always refer to some one particular or general thing, is not the universal nature of descriptive meaning, but merely one special form that the rule for that word may take. It is the simplest and most obvious form of such a rule. To use a mathematical metaphor, it makes the meaning the simplest and most obvious sort of function of the word. Our examples show that less obvious sorts of rule occur. The rule for the word 'thinking' (according to Cook Wilson) is that it means any one of the members of a certain system determined by certain epistemological facts. The rule for the term 'Swiss citizen' is that it means any one of the members of a certain system determined by certain voluntary human rules.

The rule for the word 'I' is that it is to be used by each utterer to indicate himself. (There are further elements in its rule, for example those governing the choice between 'I' and 'me'; but we need not try to state them here.)

The word 'and' is not univocal, for it has different meanings in:

(1) James and John left their nets.
(2) James and John were brothers.

But the univocity of all usages resembling the first one here lies not in any one thing of which it is the name, but in the rule: 'and' is to be used to express two sentences of the forms $Q(a)$ and $Q(b)$ in one shorter sentence, thus: $Q(a$ and $b)$.

The method of definition proper for these words is simply to state the rule of their employment, and I call it the *rule-giving* method.

Some words, when correctly used in a single usage, always refer to one and the same thing, whether a particular or a general thing. Others do not. But all words, when correctly used in a single usage, are always applied according to a single rule. In the case of 'gold', the rule is that the word is to be used only as the name of that character, gold. In the case of 'us', the rule is that the word is not to be used as the name of anything, but always to designate a group of which the speaker himself is a member. In both cases the use of the word is governed by a rule. A word that is not the name of anything is not necessarily useless; but a word without a rule of any sort to govern its usage would be quite useless. Ordinary definition deals only with words whose rule is to be a name of something. It therefore concentrates on indicating the something of which the word is a name, and assumes without mention that the rule of the word is to be a name. It tends to imply the crude view that every word is a name.

Earlier in this section I suggested that words which are not names cannot be defined by any of the previous six methods. That was an exaggeration designed to introduce the rule-giving method more easily. To write more precisely now, systematic words and demonstrative words and other

words that are not names can be defined not merely by the
rule-giving method of explicitly stating their rule, but also
by the implicative method of using them. In fact, the rule-
giving method seems to be quite rare. Apparently we learn
to use most of these words merely by observing others using
them. Children do not often ask what 'and' or 'or' or 'you' or
'who' means. The process of discovering these meanings
proceeds in silence and unselfconsciousness. And it takes
much time; Jespersen has pointed out that children are slow
to use the word 'I' not because they lack a sense of their own
personality (if they do), but because the rule for this word is
very unobvious and hard to collect from hearing people talk.
All such words *can*, however, perfectly well be defined by the
rule-giving method; and there is no reason why we may not
deliberately stipulate that a certain word is to be used not
as a name but as a systematic word, whenever we find it
convenient.

Words tend to fall into classes according to the ways in
which they are defined in common practice. There are words
that are commonly defined ostensively only, such as the
colour-words. There are words that are commonly defined
denotatively only, such as 'Romantic' in the literary sense.
(Analytic definitions of 'Romantic' are constantly being
given. But they are not effective in causing or controlling
anyone's use of the word. The only effective definition is
the naming of the persons who are pre-eminently the Roman-
tics.) There are words that are commonly defined analytically
only, such as 'billion'. There are words that are commonly
defined first ostensively and later analytically, such as 'circle'.
There are words that are commonly defined by the implicative method only, such as 'I' and 'or' and 'of'. It is not clear
whether there are words that are commonly defined only by
the synthetic method. There are probably no words that are
commonly defined by the rule-giving method only. There
are most probably no living words that are commonly defined
by the synonymous method only, because there is not much
use in a word that is only a synonym for another word. Dead
words, however, like 'buss' or 'municipium', are commonly
defined by the synonymous method only.

§ 8. The Use of Equivalences in Word-Thing Definition. Is there a method of equivalence in addition to the
methods of word-thing definition already described? A
reason for thinking so is that many logicians believe that
equivalence plays a very important part in definition. A traditional rule of logic says that the definiens must be equivalent to the definiendum or commensurate therewith, neither
broader nor narrower. Professor Ayer's book *Language*,
Truth, and Logic[1] seems to regard definition as always consisting in the statement of an equivalence, or at least always
implying an equivalence. For it seems to imply that every
definition is either an 'explicit definition' or a 'definition in
use', and it seems to say of each of these kinds that it consists
in stating an equivalence. 'We define a symbol *explicitly*
when we put forward another symbol, or symbolic expression
which is synonymous with it'; and he goes on to fix the meaning of 'synonymous' by reference to equivalence. 'We define
a symbol *in use* . . . by showing how the sentences in which
it significantly occurs can be translated into equivalent sentences which . . . .' The withdrawals made in the introduction to the second edition do not affect these points.

My answer to this question is that there is no method of
equivalence in addition to the seven methods of word-thing
definition already described, because

(1) equivalence is implied in three of those methods,
namely, the synonymous, the analytic, and the synthetic; and

(2) equivalence is not an essential part of the purpose of
word-thing definition, or of the means thereto, but
merely one means thereto that the definer may employ
if he thinks fit.

By 'equivalence' here I understand the following: two words
or expressions are equivalent if one can be substituted for
the other in any statement either without altering the truthvalue of the statement or without altering the meaning of
the statement.

1. Equivalence is implied in three of the above methods.
A synonym is an equivalent term. The expression of an

[1] 2nd ed., 1946, pp. 59–61.

analysis of a thing is equivalent to the name of the thing. And an expression giving a property or a peculiar relation of a thing, as a synthetic definition does, is equivalent to the name of the thing. Therefore equivalence is not a method distinct from those already described.

2. There seems to be a tendency to believe that the relation of equivalence is not merely a useful means that may be employed in making word-thing definitions, but is the very relation that word-thing definitions are about, so that equivalence is of the essence of word-thing definition. This tendency is probably encouraged by the expression of definitions in logical systems with the aid of the symbol ' $=$ '.

In opposition to this tendency I urge that equivalence is no part of the essence of word-thing definition, but merely an optional means of achieving word-thing definitions. For this I offer two arguments:

2.1. There are four ways in which word-thing definition can be achieved without the introduction of any equivalence, to wit, the four other methods described above. Neither the implicative nor the denotative nor the ostensive nor the rule-giving method of word-thing definition provides any symbol that is equivalent to the symbol being defined. In other words, they do not provide any definiens expression that is equivalent to the definiendum expression. This is illustrated by the following examples:

(1) implicative definition of 'diagonal': a diagonal of a square divides it into two triangles;

(2) denotative definition: 'ocean' means the Atlantic, the Pacific, &c.;

(3) ostensive definition: this (pointing to a picture) is pointilliste technique;

(4) rule-giving definition: an 'or' conjoining two statements means that at least one of them is true.

Thus it is false that the purpose of word-thing definition can be achieved only by uttering a sentence whose verb is 'is' and whose subject and predicate are equivalent and intersubstitutable expressions.

2.2. Equivalence, as we have defined it, and as almost universally understood in logic, is a relation between signs.

Only a sign can be equivalent to anything, and it can be equivalent to nothing but another sign. There are, of course, plenty of non-logical usages of the word 'equivalent', as when we say that one vitamin tablet is equivalent to three oranges. But in the logical sense of the word only symbols are equivalent to anything. Every case of logical equivalence is a relation between two signs.

In view of this, the following argument exists against the idea that word-thing definitions are about some relation of equivalence: equivalence is a relation between two or more signs, but word-thing definition is about a relation between a sign and something else that is not a sign. A word-word definition says that two expressions have the same meaning, and thus it asserts a case of equivalence. But a word-thing definition says that a certain word means a certain thing. It asserts that the relation of being-signified-by exists between this thing and this word. For example, wetness is signified by the word 'Nässe'; between the thing wetness and the word 'Nässe' there exists the relation of being-signified-by. Word-thing definition is about the relations of words not to other words but to their significates. It is the enterprise of reporting a case of meaning, of bringing a man to know that a certain word means a certain thing.

The relation of meaning, and its converse the relation of being-meant-by, are not the same as the relation of equivalence. The relation of meaning is not even a case of the relation of equivalence, for a sign and its significate are not equivalent. Dogs, for example, are not equivalent to the word 'dogs'. They are not equivalent to anything in the logical sense, because they are not signs, and only signs can be equivalent. If anything is a case of the relation of being-signified-by, then it is necessarily not a case of the relation of equivalence. Therefore word-thing definitions, being about relations of meaning, cannot be about relations of equivalence.

(Word-word definitions, however, have a very much closer relation to equivalence. At the least they always very obviously imply an equivalence, as, for example, 'the German word "rot" means the same as the French word "rouge"'. And very often they explicitly are equivalences, as, for example, 'the word "rot" is equivalent to the word "rouge"', or '$rot = rouge$'.)

Professor Ayer's use of the word 'definition' in *Language, Truth, and Logic* amounted, I think, to calling every statement of equivalence a 'definition', provided there was some interesting difference between the two expressions called equivalent (e.g. he would not call '$p = p$' a 'definition'). If, for example, it be asserted that the sentence 'the author of *Waverley* was Scotch' is equivalent to some conjunction of other sentences, then this assertion is a 'definition'. Anybody who points out that two apparently different phrases or sentences are equivalent thereby utters a 'definition'. Professor Ayer probably derived this usage from Russell; cf. 'Where a purely formal purpose is to be served, any equivalence in which a certain notion appears on one side but not on the other will do for a definition.'[1]

Is this a convenient way to use the word 'definition'? No, if the representations made in the present essay are correct. The word 'definition' is needed not merely to cover the correlation of an expression to another expression as being equivalent to it (i.e. word-word definition), but also, and more urgently, to cover the correlation of an expression to an object as being what the expression means (i.e. word-thing definition). Professor Ayer's usage neglects that most important use of the word 'definition' in which it has to do with the process by which our vocal noises come to signify the world. Furthermore, his usage adds something that ought not to be covered by the word 'definition' at all, namely, the discovery or assertion of equivalences between complete sentences as opposed to words and phrases.

§ 9. **The Definition of the Non-Indicative Functions of a Word.** I suggested earlier (Chapter III, § 4) that a word has other dimensions of meaning besides the indicative, namely, at least the expressive, the syntactic, and the contextual. But the methods of definition described in the present chapter are all methods for giving the indicative dimension of a word, or at least were described only with reference to this dimension. What are the methods for giving the function of a word in the other three dimensions? The first thing to note, in trying to answer this question, is a certain important difference between the indicative and

[1] *Principles of Mathematics*, p. 18.

the syntactic functions. Each word in a language is supposed to indicate something different (apart from the occurrence of synonyms). Thus each word is unique in its indicative function. It indicates something that no other word indicates. But the syntactical dimension is quite otherwise. A word is a noun or a verb or an adjective or one of a quite small list of other syntactical functions. Very likely we can distinguish specifically different ways of being a noun or a verb. But still very few words, if any, have a unique syntactical function, a syntactical function that no other word in the language has. It follows that the definition of the syntactical function of a word is a very easy matter: we merely mention the accepted name for that kind of function. 'Heavy' is an adjective; 'heave' is a verb.

The contextual dimension of a word is defined by the rule-giving method. One states the rule according to which the context demands or forbids the use of the word.

We define the expressive or emotional force of a word by describing as well as we can the emotion involved. The act of intentionally killing a man, for example, is called 'murder' to express extreme moral condemnation of it, 'slaughter' to express milder moral condemnation, 'liquidation' to express a minor distaste, 'killing' to express no emotion, and 'execution' to express moral approval. (These words also have, of course, some specific variations in the indicative dimension; a pair of words that differ only in their emotional function, like 'nigger' and 'negro', is rather rare.) In the simplest cases the definition of the emotional force of a word need be no more than the name of the emotion expressed plus an adverb to indicate its degree; e.g. 'mildly contemptuous'. Usually, however, the emotion expressed by a word is not one for which we have a name. Consider, for example, these two sentences:

    1. 'He is not a Christian.'
    2. 'He is a heathen.'

The second describes what the first describes, and in addition it expresses an emotion. And this emotion is not just contempt, nor just pity. It is difficult to be sure what it is; but the right account would certainly take a dozen words. The emotion we express when we call something 'obscene' is probably not mere moral condemnation; there is some kind of horror in it too.

Just as good writers are continually complicating the descriptive function of a word by metaphorical usage, so they also continually complicate the emotional function by all kinds of play that they make with our emotions. Irony is not so often *describing* a situation by words that ordinarily mean the opposite, as it is *expressing an attitude* to that situation by words that ordinarily express an opposed attitude. The dictionary-maker cannot follow all these shifts. He need not, however, assume or imply that each word has always one and the same emotional function. For often its variations are just as well marked and fixed as the variations of its descriptive senses. The word 'naïve', for example, seems regularly to express mild contempt when applied to adults, and mild delight when applied to children.

Professor C. L. Stevenson, whose discussion of emotive meaning is the best yet written, says that the emotive meaning of a word usually cannot be defined, but only characterized.[1] What he means by this is, in my language, that we usually cannot find an emotional synonym for a word, or write a phrase that is emotionally equivalent to it.

It is easy to reject this doctrine, that there are few or no emotional synonyms, for an invalid reason, namely, that we can often give a very accurate description of the emotional force of a word. That we can often give such a description is true, but does not entail that there are emotional synonyms. The error here is confusing the expression of an emotion with the description of it. The sentence 'He is sad' describes the emotion which the sentence 'Alas' expresses. The sentence 'He is greatly admiring and enjoying that' describes the emotion which the sentence 'How gorgeous' expresses. This is a true distinction in spite of the fact that, since any expression of emotion can be described, every expression of emotion suggests the description that might be given of it. It is a true distinction also in spite of the fact that, when a person describes his own present emotion, he thereby in an artificial way expresses his emotion. Description is different from the expression of emotion. The difference is hard to

[1] *Ethics and Language*, p. 82.

hold in mind when what is being described happens to be the speaker's own present emotions; but it is obvious when what is being described is not an emotion at all. Since to give a correct description of an emotion is not to express it, the fact that we probably always can give a correct description of an emotion is no evidence that there are equivalent or synonymous words or phrases in the emotional dimension of meaning.

Dictionaries have not yet described the emotion or attitude expressed by a word in any systematic way. For the most part, they have done no more than warn their readers of the words that express a shocking attitude. The main reason of this is that the distinction between the expressive and the descriptive functions of words has not been commonly held. The dictionary-makers, like nearly everyone else, have habitually regarded description as the only function of words, and therefore in their articles the expressive force of a word usually appears as part of what it describes, if it appears at all.

Yet from time to time, of course, a clear insight into the distinctness of the emotive function of words has arisen. Here is an example from the earlier eighteenth century.

'The communicating of ideas marked by words is not the chief and only end of language, as is commonly supposed. There are other ends, as the raising of some passion, the exciting to or deterring from an action, the putting the mind in some particular disposition—to which the former is in many cases barely subservient, and sometimes entirely omitted, when these can be obtained without it, and I think does not unfrequently happen in the familiar use of language. I entreat the reader to reflect with himself, and see if it does not often happen, either in hearing or reading a discourse, that the passions of fear, love, hatred, admiration, and disdain, and the like, arise immediately in his mind upon the perception of certain words, without any ideas coming between.'

That is Berkeley, writing his *Treatise Concerning the Principles of Human Knowledge*, first published in 1710.[1]

John Locke, as one result of his studies of definition, suggested that dictionary-makers might define some words by printing little pictures of the objects meant by the word. And this has come to pass. It is now time to hope that someone will take a further step, namely, write a dictionary in

[1] Introduction, § 20.

which the expressive function is explicitly distinguished, and its value determined for a great many words. There is a close approach to this proposal in the Port Royal Logic.[1]

The accurate definition of words requires us to distinguish their descriptive function from their emotional or practical functions, and give an account of each separately. The failure to do this has in the past taken the form of assuming that the whole function of words is descriptive. Consequently, this failure has done no harm in the definition of words whose practical function is non-existent or negligible; but it has led to many puzzles and errors in the definition of words whose functions are mainly practical or emotional. These puzzles have been most acute concerning the ethical words, especially 'good' and 'right'. These fascinating words are often used with almost no descriptive force, and always have a very strong evaluative or practical force. To call a thing good or an act right is not to describe the world but to intervene in it. Consequently, the attempt to define these words, being regarded as an attempt to indicate their descriptive function, always fails, because they have little or no descriptive function. (And this failure provides another ground for believing the falsehood that there are indefinable words.) What usually happens is that the words which the definer offers us as describing the thing signified by the word are really a (more or less inaccurate) description of the moral force of the word. Thus he might say that the word 'wrong' means the same as 'disapproved by me, the speaker'. This is an obvious falsehood. The descriptive function of these two terms is utterly different; or, rather, the first term 'wrong' has almost no descriptive function but a very strong emotive one; while the second term, 'disapproved by me, the speaker', has a clear descriptive function and little emotive function. The falsity of all such definitions of ethical terms has been shown again and again in the last three centuries. But they keep reappearing because they are the only way in which the emotive function of these words can achieve any form of recognition in the minds of persons who have not conceptually distinguished the emotive from the descriptive function. So overwhelming and exclusive is the emotive

---

[1] I xiii, p. 157, in *La Logique ou l'Art de Penser*, Amsterdam, 1675.

function in the case of the word 'wrong' that it must force itself on the consciousness of many definers; but, if the definer does not recognize emotive functions of words, it can do this only in the false guise of being what the word describes. Hence he will say that the word describes the speaker's disapproval. In fact the word describes almost nothing; but it expresses the speaker's disapproval, and it sets this disapproval at work on the minds of others, influencing them to act and to approve accordingly.

The *Shorter Oxford English Dictionary* comes much nearer to recognizing the emotive function of the word 'good' than of any other ethical term. It gives just such an account as one who regards the emotive function as distinct from the descriptive would give, namely, 'a term of general or indefinite commendation'; and all that is lacking is some kind of standard way of indicating that this is an account not of the descriptive but of the emotive force of the word. But the articles on 'bad', 'right', 'wrong', 'just', and 'unjust', only attempt to give words or phrases that are emotively synonymous with the word being defined; and do not give any indication that the force of the word is practical much more than descriptive.

§ 10. **The Traditional Rules of Definition.** There are certain traditional 'rules of definition', four or five or six in number, originally collected from scattered remarks in Aristotle's *Topics*, and repeated with minor variations in textbook after textbook of logic, down to at least the nineteen-thirties. Here are two twentieth-century statements of them.

The Rules of Definition according to Joseph[1]

1. A definition must give the essence of that which is to be defined.
2. A definition must be *per genus et differentiam (sive differentias)*.
3. A definition must be commensurate with that which is to be defined.
4. A definition must not, directly or indirectly, define the subject by itself.
5. A definition must not be in negative where it can be in positive terms.
6. A definition should not be expressed in obscure or figurative language.

[1] H. W. B. Joseph, *An Introduction to Logic*, 2nd ed., 1916.

The Rules of Definition according to Stebbing[1]

(reordered and renumbered for comparison with Joseph's)

3. The definiens must be equivalent to the definiendum.
4. The definiens should not include any expression that occurs in the definiendum, or that could be defined only in terms of it.
5. The definiens should not be expressed negatively unless the definiendum is negative.
6. The definiens should not be expressed in obscure or figurative language.

From the point of view that we have reached, various questions arise about these traditional rules.

1. What is the meaning of the word 'rules' here? There seem to be three possibilities. (*a*) These 'rules' might be intended in just the same way as the methods listed above, namely, as means for achieving the end or purpose of definition. (*b*) Or they might be 'rules' in the same sense as the rules of soccer, which are not methods of achieving the purpose of soccer (namely, to pass the ball through the opponent's goal) but on the contrary restrictions on the player's choice of methods to achieve this purpose. He may not, for example, carry the ball to the goal in his hands. In this case there would arise the further question why we should put restrictions on the method of defining words. A game has restrictions because it is a make-belief, and the amusement of it is produced by the artificial restrictions. But teaching people the meanings of words is a serious business, and there seems no good reason why we should rule out any efficient method of doing it. (*c*) Lastly, these 'rules' of definition might perhaps concern not the method but the purpose of definition. They might be rules as to when we should and when we should not engage in the activity of defining and pursue the end of explaining or establishing the meanings of words. So much at present for the question what the word 'rules' means here.

2. Some suspicion is aroused by the fact that these rules are described as rules of definition in general. The question arises whether there can really be any rules that are appropriate both to nominal and to real definition. It seems desirable

---

[1] L. S. Stebbing, *A Modern Introduction to Logic*, 2nd ed., 1933.

to explore the hypothesis that, in spite of the general term 'definition', they really apply only to one kind of definition. Against this, however, stands the fact that Joseph and Stebbing had four of these rules in common, although Joseph believed that definition is of things only and Stebbing believed it is of symbols only.

3. What is the evidence for these rules? How were they obtained, and what reason is there to believe that they should be followed?

The answers to these questions appear to be as follows:

Most of these rules were first written down in Aristotle's *Topics*, especially Book VI. They are not collected into one place there and presented as a list of rules, but scattered through the work along with a mass of other precepts. They have reached the twentieth century without much change except being collected together and numbered. Aristotle does not do much to recommend them by argument or explicit derivation. He mostly puts them forward as useful for the purpose in hand, implying that the reader who follows his exposition will see that they are useful, and that Aristotle has found them to be so in his full experience of the matter to which they apply. Later logicians give fewer rather than more reasons why we should follow these rules. Any cogent argument in their favour must evidently depend on definite answers to the questions what kind of definition they apply to and in what sense they are 'rules'.

A reading of the *Topics* makes it evident that Aristotle was there thinking always and only of real definition. (We must, however, make this reservation, that he was not accustomed to make the distinction between real and nominal definition; and in saying that he was thinking of real definition I do not imply that he was consciously distinguishing his subject-matter from some other subject-matter which he called 'nominal definition'.) The few passages in which Aristotle reaches or nearly reaches the notion of nominal definition are all in other works. The main subject of the *Topics* is the orderly and successful conduct of competitive disputes about essence and matters relating to essence. The sort of definition the work deals with is therefore essential or real definition.

It follows that these rules were not invented as the answer to any question about our present subject, word-thing definition. It does not follow, however, that they have no place in a discussion of word-thing definition, or that Stebbing, who held all definition to be nominal, was mistaken in introducing some of them into her discussion. Let us consider them in turn and see how each concerns real definition, and whether it has any application to word-thing definition.

1. 'A definition must give the essence of that which is to be defined' (Joseph). This of course is simply a statement of what Aristotle thought definition was. It is simply a definition of real definition as he conceived it to be. 'A definition', he says in *Topics*, I 5, 'is a statement of the essence of a thing.' This 'rule', therefore, has no connexion with nominal definition, and Stebbing was right to omit it.

2. 'A definition must be *per genus et differentiam* (*sive differentias*)' (Joseph). The original application of this was, as of all Aristotle's rules, to real definition. It meant that to find the essence of a thing one must, or at least ought to, find some genus to which the thing belongs and then find something that differentiates the thing from everything else in that genus. Can the rule be adapted in any way to word-thing definition? It would come to this, that in order to indicate the thing meant by a certain word, we ought always to give the genus and differences of that thing. To give the genus and differences of a thing is a way of analysing it. Hence this rule, if applied to word-thing definition, implies that we should never go outside the analytical method in defining words. It is therefore false if applied to word-thing definition; for we have seen that words can perfectly well be defined by other methods besides the analytical, and that some words must be otherwise defined. Stebbing was right to omit this from her list of the rules of nominal definition.

It is a very common mistake to apply this rule to word-thing definition, and demand that every word shall be explained always and only by an analysis of the thing it means. The cause of the mistake is failing to separate word-thing definition completely from real definition, failing to keep apart the two purposes, (1) to teach what thing a certain word means, and (2) to teach the essence of a thing; and hence irrationally insisting that nobody may teach what thing a certain word means without at the same time giving an analysis of the thing.

3. 'A definition must be commensurate with that which is to be defined' (Joseph). 'The definiens must be equivalent to the definiendum' (Stebbing). We have seen in a previous section of this chapter that this rule if applied to word-thing definition involves the pointless rejection of several very effective methods. It exists because Aristotle was thinking solely of real definition, of the definition of things, not words. Stebbing was mistaken in introducing it into a discussion of nominal definition.

4. 'A definition must not, directly or indirectly, define the subject by itself' (Joseph). 'The definiens should not include any expression that occurs in the definiendum, or that could be defined only in terms of it' (Stebbing). As it is often put, a definition should not be circular.

(4.1) What can this rule mean if applied to real definition? All real definitions must be capable of being expressed in words of the form 'x is yz'; and, if this form is to express something that is both true and a definition, the thing x must be the thing yz and conversely. In this sense every true real definition must define the thing by itself; and the rule appears to be the exact contradictory of the true rule. The rule can be saved only by taking it as referring to the words in which the definition is expressed. It will then be that, in defining the thing x, we must not use the word 'x' in a definiens part of our expression. In this form it is very like the rule as applied to word-thing definition, which runs: 'a definition of the word "x" must not use the word "x", but only mention it as the word being defined; nor must it use any word that can only be defined with the help of the word "x".

(4.2) What is the value of the rule in this form? The last phrase, 'nor must it use any word that can only be defined with the help of the word "x"', is useless and inoperative because there is no such word. There are no words whose definition must under all circumstances employ some particular word. There is always a choice of methods for defining any word. (Except in mathematical systems, where the restriction is deliberately made that all other terms used in the system are to be defined directly or indirectly by means of three or four terms taken as 'primitive' or 'undefined'. But this has no relevance to word-thing definition as the enterprise of teaching a man the meaning of a word; and, if this rule is intended for mathematical systems, that should be stated.)

What is the value of the rule with the last phrase removed: 'A definition of the word "x" must not use the word "x", but only mention it as the word being defined'? It is disproved by the implicative method of word-thing definition, the peculiarity of which is precisely that it defines a word by using it. 'I will tell you what "diagonal" means by telling you that every quadrilateral has two diagonals and each of them divides it into two triangles.'

This rule is sometimes expressed in the form: 'A definition must not use the word being defined or any synonym for it.' In this form it forbids the synonymous method of definition. Such a prohibition is senseless, since it is evident that a certain man may know what 'dog' means and not know what 'Hund' means, and that to such a man we can define 'Hund' by saying it means dog.

It seems as if the only truth in this rule were the trivial one that you cannot define 'dogs' by saying 'The word "dogs" means dogs', because the man who needs to have the word 'dogs' defined for him will not understand such a sentence. But there is slightly more to it than this; and, as commonly in such cases, the key lies in confining our attention to the analytical method of definition, which is the only method that traditional logic has in mind most of the time. What the rule intends to say is that the analytical method of definition, 'x is yz', cannot succeed if either 'y' or 'z' is a synonym for 'x' or is itself the name of something analysable into x and something else. In either of those cases 'x is yz' is not an analysis or not a true analysis of the thing x, and therefore does not provide a means of successfully defining the word 'x' by the analytical method. Circularity is a disease of analysis, not of definition. It is the disease of analysis that consists in representing a thing as being a synthesis of elements one of which is itself.

5. 'A definition must not be in negative where it can be

in positive terms' (Joseph). 'The definiens should not be expressed negatively unless the definiendum is negative' (Stebbing). The origin and history of this curious rule might be interesting to search out. Alone of the six, it does not seem to occur in Aristotle.[1] What answer would the logicians give if we suggested that every truth can be expressed either affirmatively or negatively and asked why they imply that some facts cannot be stated in affirmative language and why they hold that all definitions are better stated in affirmative language if possible? Is it a matter of style that they have in mind, that it is better style to say a thing is 'considerable' than to say it is 'not inconsiderable', just as it is commonly more effective to use the active than the passive voice? Or are they pointing out the very obvious fact that one cannot say what a thing is by mentioning something that it is not, and one cannot say what a word means by mentioning something that it does not mean? Perhaps so, for some great writers seem to have gone against this fact. It is true that a point has no parts; but when Euclid offers 'a point is that which has no parts' as a 'definition' he seems to imply that this statement can give us either the analysis of a point or the meaning of the word 'point' or both, which it cannot. Possibly the origin of this rule is connected with Plato's method of reaching definitions by division, that is, by assigning the thing to be defined to a genus and then dividing this genus into parts. It does not appear, however, that Plato thought of this division as always or even often into a term and its negative. Whatever its origin may be, the rule can stand only as a warning that when we try to say what the analysis of a given thing is we sometimes merely say that it is not something or other, and when we try to say what a given word means we sometimes merely say that it does not mean so and so. It is simply a warning against a type of failure which seems too elementary to occur but nevertheless does sometimes occur.

6. 'A definition should not be expressed in obscure or figurative language' (Joseph). 'The definiens should not be expressed in obscure or figurative language' (Stebbing).

---

[1] *Topics*, VI 4, on defining things through their opposites, e.g. good through evil, does not appear to contain it.

Obscurity sometimes has good results, but the increase of knowledge among men is never one of them. From the point of view of spreading knowledge, either of the essences of things by real definition or of the meanings of words by nominal definition, obscurity should always be avoided and clarity maximized. The advice is sound but very obvious. Why has it been enshrined in a 'rule' rather than many other equally sound and equally obvious pieces of general advice? Perhaps because several obscure and useless sentences have imposed themselves in our literature as profound real definitions.

The ban on figurative language is included in the same rule as the warning against obscurity probably because the fault of figures is thought to be their obscurity. They can be obscure. They are perhaps more often uncertain and ineffective than obscure. On the other hand, figures of speech are vague and implicit analogies; and analogy in its precise form may achieve the purpose of word-thing definition because it may set the thing meant by the word in a unique relation and thus become a synthetic or an implicit definition. Aristotle defined the word 'matter' figuratively and successfully when he said that matter is to substance what the bronze is to the statue.

To sum up this review, the first three rules would be grossly false if applied to word-thing definition. The fourth is mostly false, but has a mite of truth if reinterpreted and restricted to the analytical method. The fifth and sixth are warnings against very obvious forms of failure in definition. The whole spirit of these rules is for two reasons quite foreign to my purpose in this chapter, which is to consider how word-thing definitions can succeed. The first reason for this inappropriateness is that the rules are derived from a work, the *Topics* of Aristotle, which is never concerned with nominal definition but only with real definition. The other reason is that the rules are derived from a work which is concerned not with teaching and learning and the spread of knowledge, but with competitive disputation and the achievement of victory in argument. Competition and strife can have their pleasures preserved and their pains diminished by making the participants submit to artificial restrictions or 'rules'. The whole idea of laying down 'rules' for definition is an inappropriate survival from the competitive atmosphere of Aristotle's *Topics*.

The mathematicians have a tradition about rules of definition which appears to be unrelated to the Aristotelian tradition and much younger. It can be found, for example, in Walther Dubislav's *Die Definition*, pp. 34–8, and in Alfred Tarski's *Introduction to Logic*, pp. 35, 133, 150. It is concerned with the use of definitions in mathematical systems, where the object is not to teach the reader a new usage but to construct an elegant and logical system in which nearly all the terms are capable of being replaced by longer expressions consisting wholly of a few so-called 'primitive' terms. This 'systematic definition', as we may baptize it, is so different from our nominal definition that the job of teaching the reader what the terms in the system mean often has to be done by 'remarks' which are outside the system. I shall say some more about it in Chapter VII on definition in systems.

VI

REAL DEFINITION

§ 0. Many Persons have believed in Real Definition. The previous chapters, except the first, have been about the definition of words. According to a vast number of excellent thinkers, there is also another kind of definition, namely, the definition of things. The inventors of the notion of definition, Socrates and Plato, were obviously thinking only of the definition of things and not at all of the definition of words. The search for the definition of piety in Plato's *Euthyphro* is certainly an inquiry about the thing piety, not about the word 'piety'. Socrates does not ask Euthyphro what piety is because the word 'piety' is new to him, or because he cannot think of an effective method of teaching the use of this word to those who do not know it. He is not asking a question about the word 'piety', but using the word 'piety' to ask a question about the thing piety. He assumes that both he and Euthyphro already know the use of the word. The subject-matter of the dialogue falls within the field of ethics, not that of linguistics or lexicography. The same is certainly true of every other place in Plato's writings where there is discussion of a question having the form 'What is *x*?', that is to say, a request for a definition. 'What is justice?' and 'What is imitation?' in the *Republic*, 'What is courage?' in *Laches*, 'What is temperance?' in *Charmides*, 'What is knowledge?' and 'What is logos?' in *Theaetetus*, 'What is the soul?' in *Phaedo*, 'What is the sophist?' in the *Sophist*—in these and all the other cases the question is about a thing, not about a word.

Aristotle's definitions of motion as the actualization of the potential as potential, of time as the number of motion in respect of before and after, of happiness as the activity of the soul &c., of virtue as a habit of choice &c., were certainly not intended by him to be about words. He defines definition as the statement that gives the essence. Essence of what? He certainly did not mean essence of a word.

Spinoza in Part Three of his *Ethics* gradually collects, and then lists altogether at the end, forty-eight definitions of human emotions. It seems quite evident that he intended them to be definitions of the emotions, not of the words for emotions. '*Love* is joy with the accompanying idea of an external cause.' '*Timidity* is the desire of avoiding a dreaded greater evil by means of a lesser one.' Those are not nominal definitions of the words 'timidity' and 'love'. Spinoza is neither legislating a new meaning for these words nor reporting an old one. He is using an old meaning to talk about the emotions themselves. Earlier in the work he writes that 'the true definition of each thing involves nothing and expresses nothing but the nature of the thing defined'.[1]

This assumption that there is definition of things, often appearing in the extreme form that all definition is of things, is constantly found not only in the greatest thinkers like Plato, Aristotle, and Spinoza, but in a host of lesser men also. To mention two or three random examples: Cook Wilson in his *Statement and Inference* was clearly talking about real definition all the time, and thought this too obvious to be worth mentioning, and thought it too obvious to be worth stating that real definition occurs and is important, while nominal definition is unimportant. John Dewey wrote: 'Many definitions of mind and thinking have been given. I know of but one that goes to the heart of the matter:— response to the doubtful as such.'[2] Evidently this cannot be and is not intended to be a definition of the *word* 'mind'. When Professor Perry says that 'the problem of comparative value ⟨is⟩ a problem of definition rather than of attribution',[3] he must mean real and not nominal definition; he could not think that his 694 pages were concerned with the nominal definition of the word 'value'.

The belief that there is such a thing as indefinability usually involves the assumption that there is such a thing as real definition. While a few people have held that there are indefinable *words*, owing to their narrow interpretation of nominal definition, most of those who have believed in indefinables have regarded them as indefinable *things*, things, that is, to which in their opinion one cannot apply the pro-

---

[1] *Ethics*, I, prop. 8, n. 2.   [2] *The Quest for Certainty*, p. 214.
[3] *General Theory of Value*, p. 596; and he says the same of the problem of generic value.

cess of real definition, whatever they conceived that to be. Thus Professor Moore in *Principia Ethica* held that the thing goodness is indefinable, because 'definitions which describe the real nature of the object or notion denoted by a word, and which do not merely tell us what the word is used to mean, are only possible when the object or notion in question is something complex'.[1]

Another common belief about definition, which usually involves the assumption that definition is of things, is the belief that definitions can and should be proved. Proof is something quite inappropriate to a legislative nominal definition, because such a definition is not a statement. A dictionary nominal definition is a statement and can properly be proved; large dictionaries offer evidence, namely, quotations, for the meanings they assign to words. But a great many of the persons who say or imply that definitions should be demonstrated are obviously not thinking of anything like the evidence offered in a dictionary, but of some more or less *a priori* process of deduction. Thus Plato in the *Sophist* regarded his new method of division as a means of proving a definition. Aristotle devotes a large part of his *Posterior Analytics* to the question how definitions can be proved, evidently feeling that they ought to be; and in various parts of his works he offers evidence and argument in support of particular real definitions that he gives, for examples that of happiness in *Nicomachean Ethics* I, and that of motion in *Physics* III 1 and 2. Frege in his *Foundations of Arithmetic* obviously and overwhelmingly regards definitions as propositions to be discovered and proved; they require confirmation and logical justification, and this must be something better than merely showing that the definition has not yet led to a contradiction. Professor Perry offers evidence for the truth of his definition of value (ch. V). In all of these men what is to be proved is not that the English use the word 'time' to mean *tempus*, or anything of that sort, but that the thing time is of a certain nature.

I will mention a third common belief about definition which also seems to imply that definition is of things: the belief that definition should come at the end of a book or

[1] *Principia Ethica*, p. 7.

discussion, not at the beginning. Kant said that philosophical definition should come at the end. Mr. Carritt in his *Theory of Beauty* said generally that definition should come at the end. When we ask whether these doctrines refer to nominal or to real definition, it seems evident that nominal definitions should *not* come at the end of a discussion. The only exception to this would be when the purpose of the discussion is philological, to ascertain, for example, what the Romans meant by the word '*gravitas*'. And even then it might be better to state one's answer before as well as after the discussion. But when the point of defining a word in a discussion is, as usual, to use the word in that discussion, then it would be most ineffective to defer the definition of the word until you had finished using the word. The doctrine that definition should come at the end is therefore quite implausible if applied to nominal definition, and therefore those who maintain it are evidently believing that there is such a thing as real definition.

We have now established the historical fact that many people believe that there is such a thing as the definition of things, and we must ask whether this belief is true. My answer is that the search for real definitions, as initiated by Socrates and continued down to to-day, has not been one single kind of activity; it has included several different sorts of activity; its practitioners have not distinguished these differences, but regarded them all as the one thing, definition; and of these activities at least one is wholly bad, because it assumes something false; while others are bad in the confused state in which they appear under the head of definition, but can be good if disentangled. I shall describe each of these activities in turn, or rather as many of them as I can distinguish. All of them are already pretty evident in the works of Plato.

§ 1. **Real Definition as the Search for a Non-existent Identity of Meaning.** The search for real definitions has often been, unknown to its practitioners, an insistence on discovering some identity in all the applications of an ambiguous word. A word like 'virtue' has been taken; a brief survey made of habits to which it is applied; and then the demand made that we shall state what it is that is common to all these habits by reason of which they all, and they only, are called 'virtues'. This is very often the nature of real definition in Plato's dialogues. In his *Meno* we find Socrates insisting with absolute confidence that of course virtue must be the same in every case.[1]

This activity is bad, of course, in any event, whether confused with a study of things or understood in its true nature. All words are ambiguous; and we are bound to make falsehoods if we start by insisting without investigation that some particular word has only one sense. Not that we ought never to seek for a single meaning in several applications that at first sight appear to be ambiguous; there often is a hidden identity, and we should try hard to find it. But we should always have in mind the probability of ambiguity, and the flexible nature of our vocabulary which causes it. The error of assuming that most of our abstract terms are univocal will probably never be made again on so grand a scale by so great and educated a mind as it is in the early and middle dialogues of Plato; but lesser manifestations of it will probably occur as long as there are human beings. And every man who seeks a real definition of the thing *x* ought to ask himself first whether he has good reason to believe that he is referring to not more than one thing by his word '*x*'. Until we have isolated and chosen a single sense of the word '*x*', it is necessarily misleading to start asking for a real definition of the thing *x*. If the sentence '*x* is *yz*' expresses a significant real definition, then the word '*x*' in this sentence must mean something, and not more than one thing, to the hearer apart from the predicate. For if the word '*x*' does not mean anything to him before the sentence is uttered, it is not a real definition but a nominal definition of the word '*x*'; while if the word '*x*' means more than one thing in this sentence, it is a muddle. This is the truth that Pascal expressed epigrammatically by saying that, 'if someone says "time is the motion of a creature", we must ask him what he means by this word "time"' (285).

§ 2. **Real Definition as the Search for Essence.** Secondly, the search for real definitions has often been the search for essences. Definition was defined by Aristotle as the statement of the essence of a thing, and both he and Plato always

---

[1] I have discussed his curious argument in *Plato's Earlier Dialectic*, p. 59.

conceived of definition as such. On this interpretation, if
'*x* is *yz*' is a significant and true real definition of *x*, then *x* is
a thing and *yz* is the essence of that thing. 'A definition', said
Spinoza, 'if it is to be called perfect, must explain the inmost
essence of a thing.'[1]

This activity of searching for essence is bad because there
is no such thing as essence in the sense intended. We can
convince ourselves of this by studying the most serious
attempt there has ever been to make sense of the notion of
essence, namely, Aristotle's *Metaphysics Z* 4–6. In these be-
wildering chapters we find Aristotle reaching the mysterious
conclusions that some things have an essence and others do
not, and that of the things that do have an essence some are
the same as their essence and others are not. These doctrines,
and the very great obscurity of the chapters, suggest strongly
that there is a muddle somewhere. If a man asks Aristotle
what he means by the word 'essence' (τὸ τί ἐστι, τὸ τί ἦν
εἶναι), the nearest Aristotle comes to a reply is to say that
an essence is what is stated in a definition.[2] This would help
if we knew what a definition was, but according to Aristotle
a definition is a statement of essence. A definition states
essence, and essence is what you find in a definition. This
useless circle is the best that can be extracted from Aristotle
when we ask what he meant by 'essence', and it is strong
evidence that there is no such thing as essence in his sense
of the word.

Yet there has been from Plato onwards a very strong and
persistent tendency to believe in essence. In particular, it
has been a tendency to believe in the distinction between
essence and property. A property, says Aristotle, is a predicate which does not indicate the essence of a thing, but yet
belongs to that thing alone, and is predicated convertibly of
it.[3] And people argue that being bounded by three sides is
certainly the essence of a triangle rather than a property,
while having the sum of its interior angles equal to half a turn
is certainly a property and not the essence of a triangle. This
argument shows where the confusion lies and why the belief
in essence persists. It is once again the confusion of real

[1] *Improvement of the Understanding*, van Vloten & Land I 31.
[2] 1029ᵇ20.   [3] *Topics*, I 5.

definition with nominal definition, in the form of wrongly taking a case of word-thing definition to be a case of real definition. That being bounded by three sides is the essence and not a property of the triangle is merely a confused way of saying that we define the word 'triangle' to mean a figure bounded by three sides. That having the sum of its interior angles equal to half a turn is a property and not the essence of the triangle is merely a confused way of saying that this characteristic is not assigned to be the meaning of the word 'triangle', but entails and is entailed by another characteristic which *is* assigned to be the meaning of the word 'triangle'. If we choose, there is nothing in the world to prevent us from defining the word 'triangle' to mean a figure whose interior angles sum to half a turn; and then this would be the essence of a triangle, while its having three sides would be a property.

Essence, then, is just the human choice of what to mean by a name, misinterpreted as being a metaphysical reality. The essence of x is the proposition that 'the word "x" is defined to mean yz', misunderstood as the proposition that 'x is yz', where the expressions 'x' and 'yz' are thought to have different meanings, although in reality they have the same meaning because the expression 'x' is defined as meaning yz.

Another reason why the belief in essence persists is that it is always plausible to ask a question of the form 'What is x?', and it is thought that the answer will be the essence of x. But discussion of the 'What is x?' type of question had better be postponed until later.

The doctrine of essence, though still much alive in general, is now dead among logicians. One of its dying gasps may be observed in H. W. B. Joseph's *Introduction to Logic*. He abandons it entirely outside the sphere of geometry; e.g. 'the problem of distinguishing between essence and property in regard to organic kinds may be declared insoluble' (102). But he retains it in its original home, geometry. 'The essence of any species of figure includes so much as need be stated in order to set the figure as it were before us' (96). A circle has a larger area than any other plane figure of equal perimeter. But that cannot be the essence of circle, *because it does not without further demonstration enable us to visualize the figure intended* (98). Thus the essence is that property which immediately enables us to visualize the figure! Joseph does not remark that in this case many things inside geometry lack essence as well as all things outside. For there is an infinity of figures which, owing to their complexity, cannot be visualized at all as such. No one can visualize a chiliagon so as to distinguish it from a myriagon.

§ 3. **Real Definition as Description plus Naming.** The two activities so far described are wholly bad and should be entirely dropped. But I come now to other activities, also passing under the title of 'real definition', which can be legitimate and desirable, provided they are distinguished from each other and from the wholly bad forms of real definition.

Consider these two sentences:

1. 'The essence of egotism is the inability to regard anything but oneself as real.'
2. 'There are people who cannot regard anything but themselves as real.'

The second is an existential statement, an assertion that a certain character sometimes occurs. I suggest that the first is often just another way of saying what the second says. In general, I suggest that the form of statement 'x is yz', or 'the definition of x is yz', or 'the essence of x is yz', is often just a way of asserting that yz is something that occurs. In other words, a real definition is often an existential proposition in disguise.

An amusing example of this occurs in Nicholas Steno's *Elementorum Myologiae Specimen, seu Musculi Descriptio Geometrica*, published in 1657. Under the influence of his century's passion for geometrical method, Steno was led to represent the following anatomical description as a definition:

Def. 1. Fibra Motrix est minutissimarum fibrillarum sibi mutuo secundum longitudinem immediate iunctarum certa compages, cuius intermedia pars ab extremis differt consistentia, crassitie, et colore, et ab intermedia parte vicinarum fibrarum motricium separata est per transversas fibrillas propriae musculorum membranae continuas.

The crass unsuitability of the Euclidean manner to a description of the body is reflected in the fact that Steno has 44 definitions and five suppositions to only six lemmata and one proposition.

Many so-called 'real definitions', of the form 'x is yz', are equivalent to the statement that: 'The character yz occurs, and I call this character (or it is commonly called) by the name "x".'

It is a legitimate and useful activity to point out that a certain character occurs, and to give it a name or report its accepted name. On the other hand, it is mere loss to call this activity 'real definition'; for that can only conjure up the wraith of essence or at least confuse the activity with some of the other activities called 'real definition'. The proper description of it is that it is an existential proposition plus a nominal definition. The nominal definition assigns a short name to the character described at greater length in the existential proposition. If we need an abbreviation for this, we can stipulate some name less confusing than 'real definition'.

§ 4. **Real definition as Word-thing Definition Misconceived.** Fourthly, real definition has often been, unknown to its practitioners, wholly or in part, word-thing definition misconceived. They have often supposed themselves to be studying a thing when they were in fact seeking a method of nominally defining a word. We often know the meaning of a word without having at our immediate disposal any method of teaching its meaning to someone else. Then we may seek for a form of words that would embody a method of teaching the meaning, whether a case of the synonymous or of the analytic or of the synthetic or of any other verbal method of achieving word-thing definitions. Or we may insist on using only the analytic method, and then our supposed study of the nature of a thing is in fact a search for an analytical method of teaching the meaning of the name of that thing. This confusion between an attempt to understand the nature of a thing, and an attempt to convey the meaning of a word by the analytical method, explains the fact that we often find language suitable only to word-thing definition in the works of those who repudiate nominal definition and profess to practise only real definition. Thus Spinoza, who is thoroughly realistic in his view of definition, nevertheless expresses his most important definitions by such phrases as: 'By substance I understand that which . . . (Per substantiam intelligo id quod . . .).' This phrase means nothing unless the word 'substance' is taken to be here meant in inverted commas, as the name of itself. But then it is about a word, not about a thing. One can understand something by a word; but one can understand nothing by a thing, unless it is a symbol or a pair of spectacles or something of that sort.

Similarly Aristotle, another realist in the theory of definition, while he takes himself to be saying that the *thing* actuality is indefinable, is in fact saying that he cannot teach the reader what he means by the *word* 'actuality' by the analytical method of word-thing definition, and betrays this by using phrases like 'what I mean' (ὃ βουλόμεθα λέγειν).[1]

This sort of supposed real definition is, then, an activity which is undesirable when misconceived as definition of things, but very desirable when taken for what it is, the definition of words by the analytical method. The value of the word-thing definition of words by the analytical method is great; but the value of a confused version of this, regarded as not about the word but about the thing, is nil.

§ 5. **Real Definition as a Tautology obtained directly from a Nominal Definition.** A man might make the following two utterances in succession:

1. 'I stipulate that in my future utterances the word "triangle" is to be taken as meaning a three-sided rectilinear area.'
2. 'A triangle is a three-sided rectilinear area.'

Then, in view of his first utterance, his second utterance is a tautology. It is necessarily true, and its truth follows from its meaning alone. There is no need to investigate the world in order to discover whether his second utterance is true. There is no need, for example, to discuss whether we live in a Euclidean space. The world can be what it likes, and change as it chooses; but that a triangle is a three-sided rectilinear area remains an eternal truth. In order to determine the truth or falsity of a statement, we always have to know

[1] *Metaphysics, Θ 6.*

what it means, and we usually have to know also something about the world. Thus, in order to determine the truthvalue of 'Stags shed their antlers once a year', we must first find out what it means, and then watch stags. But there are some statements for which only the first is necessary. For examples, the statements 'stags are stags' and 'stags are not stags'. In order to know whether these are true or false, we need only know what they mean. A statement which must be false by its meaning alone, no matter what the world is like, is a contradiction; and a statement which must be true by its meaning alone, no matter what the world is like, is a tautology.

Many nominal definitions immediately suggest a tautology. For example, if we define the word 'buss' by the synonymous method of saying 'the word "buss" means a kiss', that suggests the tautology 'a buss is a kiss'. All word-thing definitions by the analytical method suggest a tautology. Whenever we define the word 'x' to mean the compound yz, we suggest the tautology 'x is yz'.

Such apprehension of a statement as following directly from a nominal definition (if 'following' is a good word for this peculiar relation) is often misconceived by those who possess it, and falsely supposed to be a discovery about the nature of the world. This is clear from the fact that they will offer facts about the world as evidence for the truth of their statement. The only correct evidence for the above statement that 'a triangle is a three-sided rectilinear area' is that 'I have defined the word "triangle" to mean a three-sided rectilinear area'. To offer any other evidence is irrelevant, and shows that the speaker has not understood the nature of his own mental activity.

Many people offer factual evidence for the proposition that 'all actions are aimed at the doer's own purposes' (which I will call 'egoism'), and insist that egoism is absolutely certain. But, if egoism is absolutely certain, it is so merely because we define 'my purpose' to mean what I am aiming at. And the correct defence of the proposition is simply to point out that it is a mere tautology, and not a factual statement about human nature. Whenever we find a person absolutely confident about some very sweeping statement, it

is wise to investigate whether the statement is true by definition and empty of factual importance, even if its upholder
believes it to be a valuable piece of psychology or other
positive science.

Professor C. I. Lewis's doctrine that the *a priori* is defini-
tory[1] is, I presume, equivalent to the doctrine that all *a priori*
truths are tautologies generated by word-thing definitions.

The name 'real definition' has sometimes meant a tautology of the form '*x* is *yz*', following immediately from a word-
thing definition of the word '*x*' as meaning the compound *yz*,
when this tautology has been misconceived as a factual statement. For example, Dr. Suzanne Mansion thinks that the
real definition 'man is a rational animal' is a factual statement, although she mentions on the same page the nominal
definition that 'the animal that has reason is called "man"'.
The same error is present less obviously when she writes:

'When, for example, after having explained the meaning of the term
triangle, one proves that the triangle exists, its definition, from having
been nominal, becomes real; but its tenor remains identical: it contains
the same marks as before, without addition or alteration. Nevertheless
the import of these two definitions is profoundly different, since only
the second attains anything real.'[2]

Such a use of the phrase 'real definition' is obviously
undesirable and should be dropped, since it involves an error,
namely, mistaking a tautology for a statement about reality.
'Real definition' is not a suitable name for a tautology.

On the other hand, it is very desirable that we should
distinguish between an analytic word-thing definition and
the tautology to which it gives rise. The failure to do so has
led to statements like this: 'The statement that one and one
make two simply records our decision as to what to mean
by the word "two".' If that were true, mathematics would
be a record or history of human decisions as to the use of
words, and therefore a part of lexicography. Mathematics
is not a part of lexicography, because the tautology, that one
and one make two, is not the same thing as the word-thing
definition on which it is based, that the word 'two' means

---

[1] *Mind and the World Order, passim.*

[2] My translations from *Le Jugement d'existence chez Aristote*, Louvain,
1946, pp. 260–1, 268.

one and one. The definition is about a word; but the mathematical proposition is not.

§ 6. Real Definition as the Search for the Cause.

Sixthly, the search for the real definition of a thing has often been the search for the cause of that thing, for the conditions under which it will necessarily occur. Aristotle defined happiness as activity in accordance with complete virtue, sufficiently equipped with external goods, and not for some chance period but throughout a complete life. Evidently this is not what the word 'happiness' means nor what the thing happiness is. It is the circumstances under which Aristotle thinks happiness will occur. It is his suggestion as to how to become happy.

In Plato's and Aristotle's circles there was discussion of various definitions of pleasure, such as 'pleasure is a perceptible transition to the natural state'. Evidently these so-called 'definitions' were theories of the conditions under which pleasure occurs. The example given would be more properly expressed: 'Pleasure occurs when and only when the body is passing from an unnatural to the natural state, and the transition occurs fast enough to be perceived.' Certainly the word 'pleasure' does not mean a perceptible transition to the natural state, and certainly this phrase cannot possibly give a correct analysis of that state of feeling which we call 'pleasure'.

For a third example, Plato's definition of righteousness or δικαιοσύνη in the *Republic* is in part, though not wholly, a theory of the conditions under which righteous behaviour will occur. A man will act righteously, Plato declares, when and only when each of the parts of his soul is doing its proper business and not meddling with the business of other parts. He will act unrighteously when and only when some part of his soul is not doing, or not only doing, its own business.

In one place Aristotle explicitly demands that definitions shall give the cause. This passage fails to distinguish cause from premiss, and it asks that definitions give the cause *as well as* the 'what'; nevertheless it is a good illustration of the conception of real definition which I am now describing:

'Our defining statement ought not merely to give the fact, as most definitions do. The cause should also be contained in it and appear. But the actual formulations of definitions are like conclusions. For example: "What is squaring? It is making an equilateral rectangle equal in area to an oblong one." Such a definition is a statement of the conclusion. But one which says "squaring is the discovery of a mean" gives the cause of the matter.'[1]

Thus in Plato and Aristotle the so-called 'definition' of *x* was often in fact the cause of *x*; and the search for definitions, the struggle to answer the question 'What is *x*?', was a misguided form of the search for causes. The same is true of hundreds of real definitions since. In manuals of educational psychology, for example, the question 'What is learning?' is often really a search for the conditions of learning, for a mechanism by which people may be brought to learn more and to learn faster. If Spinoza used the word 'cause' in the ordinary sense, he had this kind of definition in mind when he laid it down as a rule for definitions of creatures that they must 'comprehend the proximate cause'.[2]

The search for causes is of course a legitimate and extremely valuable activity. But nothing is gained by thinking of it as a search for definitions. It is a dead loss to pursue the question what are the conditions of *x* under the impression that one is seeking the definition or essence of *x*. It tends to prevent one from making the empirical tests that are appropriate to all theories about causes.

§ 7. Real Definition as the Search for a Key. Mr. Santayana, in his book on *The Sense of Beauty*, made the following extremely large demands on real definition:

'A definition ⟨of beauty⟩ that should really define must be nothing less than the exposition of the origin, place, and elements of beauty as an object of human experience. We must learn from it, as far as possible, why, when, and how beauty appears, what conditions an object must fulfil to be beautiful, what elements of our nature make us sensible of beauty, and what the relation is between the constitution of the object and the excitement of our sensibility. Nothing less will really define beauty or make us understand what aesthetic appreciation is. The definition of beauty in this sense will be the task of this whole book, a task that can be only very imperfectly accomplished within its limits.'

One phrase of this suggests that Mr. Santayana's defini-

---

[1] *De anima*, II 2, 413[a]13–20.
[2] *Improvement of the Understanding*, p. 32, van Vloten & Land.

tion of beauty is nothing less than his whole book on beauty; and it may be hard to believe that anything shorter could accomplish all that he here demands a definition shall do. Yet there is a persistent tradition that a definition must be something brief, something certainly not more than a paragraph, and preferably not more than a sentence. Cicero introduced the word 'short' into his definition of definition. Is Mr. Santayana simply disregarding this tradition? I think not. For the tradition is that a definition, while being very small itself, shall serve as the key to a very large building. The search for the real definition of *x* has often been the attempt to compress all the facts about *x* into a single short phrase. Thus when a man asks 'What is Christianity?' or 'What is the essence of Jesus's message?', he is often hoping that every precept which Jesus taught follows from some one precept which he taught.

Spinoza was thinking of definition in this way in his second rule for the definition of creatures:

'A conception or definition of a ⟨created⟩ thing should be such that all the properties of that thing, in so far as it is considered by itself, and not in conjunction with other things, can be deduced from it, as may be seen in the above definition of a circle ⟨the figure described by any line of which one end is fixed and the other free⟩. . . . That this is a necessary characteristic of a definition is so clear to anyone, who reflects on the matter, that there is no need to spend time in proving it.'[1]

Such was 'the real, adequate, genetic definition that Spinoza desiderates, which possesses in itself, and in its intrinsic sources, the *nisus* of its own development', to quote his interpreter Hallett.[2] (Hallett seems almost to want to ascribe to Spinoza the view that we can actually create things by giving definitions in accordance with his rules; cf. 'the adequately defined circle or sphere is real because it generates its own properties'.)

But is it possible to compress all the facts about *x* into a single short phrase? It is possible if there is some one fact about *x* from which everything else about *x* necessarily follows. Accordingly, the search for the real definition of *x* has often been the attempt to find some one fact about *x* from which everything else that is true of *x* can be deduced.

[1] *Improvement of the Understanding*, ibidem.　　[2] *Mind*, 1942, pp. 141, 143.

People have been confident that this is possible because they were sure that it happens in geometry. Everything we know about the triangle, they said, follows from the one little fact that the triangle is a plane figure bounded by three straight lines. If this can be done with the triangle, why not with justice, with religion, with life, with individuality, with everything? For every object there must be, if we could only find it, a single little definition from which every truth about that object follows.

What is the value of this activity? The possession of a small key to a large building is obviously valuable. If a large body of knowledge can be inferred from a single sentence, we should by all means try to discover that sentence. And it is true that this can sometimes be done; for it has been done in mathematics. It is the process called 'axiomatization', presenting a large body of propositions and showing that a small part of them, called the 'axioms' or 'postulates', entail all the rest.

But it cannot always be done. Here, for example, are two facts about the triangle that cannot be deduced from its definition: the triangle was studied by Euclid, and John thinks triangles more beautiful than squares.

Can we say that the activity is suitable only to logical and mathematical matters and inapplicable to all matters of occurrence? Probably not. Professor Dubs urges that essential definitions (his name for definitions that enable us to deduce all the properties of the thing defined) are the goal of natural science. The 'nuclear equation' for the simpler elements, he says, especially hydrogen, is the beginning of an essential definition.[1] We cannot exclude the possibility that we may find definitions of the elementary particles of matter, from which, together with certain quite general laws, we may be able to deduce all the properties of the elements and compounds.

But what is clear is that such definitions must include, or be preceded by, a legislative nominal element. It is no good looking for a real definition of religion from which to deduce all religious occurrences, until we have subjected the word 'religion' to some stipulative redefinition. For the word

[1] *Philosophical Review*, 1943.

'religion' as it stands is attached to reality in various ways. Some people exclude morality from religion. Some make morality the whole of religion. It is most unlikely that any definition could generate all the types of occurrence actually covered by the common usage of the word, because it is most unlikely that the word covers only one homogeneous field. The definition of the triangle generates all the properties of the triangle only because the word 'triangle' is formally restricted to the definition given by a deliberate choice which need not coincide with actual usage; and occurrences are not envisaged or referred to except in so far as they may happen to embody the pattern defined. A definition of religion, on the other hand,[1] professes to be about occurrences, about the actual prayer and worship of actual persons. When we are dealing with a common word of wide application, like the word 'religion', no real or essential definition of the thing meant is likely to be a true key to the area covered, until this area has been inspected piece by piece, the affinities of its parts ascertained, and the meaning of the word judiciously narrowed and explicitly announced. The physicists and chemists made systematic investigations for many years before reaching their essential definitions of the simpler parts of matter. The anthropologist does the same with religion.

The conclusion is that real definition as a search for a small key to a large area is a possible and valuable activity, but not one to be attempted lightly or hastily, and always requiring to be accompanied by nominal redefinition of the term used.

Should it be called 'real definition'? Probably not. Besides the general reason for not calling any of these activities 'real definition' (namely, that to do so confuses them with each other), this name tends to conceal the large probability that there is no simple key to the subject-matter. Probably it is undesirable here to use any phrase shorter than: 'I am trying to find some element on which all the rest of this matter depends, but I do not know whether there is such a thing.'

§ 8. **Real Definition as the Adoption and Recommendation of Ideals.** The search for real definitions is sometimes,

---

[1] As in F. H. Bradley's *Appearance and Reality*, 1930, pp. 388–9.

eighthly, a search for ideals, an endeavour to choose what things to value and what flag to follow; and the announcement of real definitions is sometimes the announcement of one's allegiance and the act of persuading others to adopt the same ideals. Thus when Plato asks 'What is justice?', and concludes with elaborate procedures and ceremonies that it is each part's minding its own business, this is among other things a confession that Plato values rank and station and order above other things in politics, and a strong emotional influence directed towards his readers to get them to adopt the same ideal. The word 'justice' is suited for such evaluating and influencing by its strong moral tone. This moral tone is not an accidental association in the minds of a few users of the word. It is a permanent association in the minds of all its users, and hence may properly be called part of its meaning. It is the evaluative meaning of the word, as opposed to any descriptive meaning it may have. And the effect of saying that 'the true definition of justice is yz' is to make people, in so far as they accept your suggestion, apply the evaluative tone of the word 'justice' to the thing described by the words 'yz'.

A very large proportion of the words that have been subjected to intensive real definition are words in the meaning of which some non-descriptive, evaluative element is prominent. In Plato's dialogues they nearly all are so, with the possible exception of 'knowledge'; for nearly all of them are obviously moral terms, and of the rest at least the following have a strong evaluative element in them: 'sophist', 'statesman', 'imitation', 'friendship'.

A definition of democracy is usually an attempt to find, in the sphere of government, the ideal state of things, or the best constitutional means of approaching the ideal, it being already agreed that this ideal includes or involves a large participation of the common people in the forming of public policy. Often this limitation is omitted, and the definition of democracy comes to be the most general attempt to state the ideal constitution, whatever that may be. This is especially common among persons to the left of Liberalism. Thus Mr. R. H. S. Crossman defined democracy as not necessarily involving representative institutions:

'The democratic faith is not tied to any political or social system. It regards all systems (including "democracy") as instruments for the self-realization of human nature; and if representative institutions are shown to be no longer useful for that purpose, then the democrat must look elsewhere for other instruments and better institutions.'[1]

Marx wrote that the value of commodities is constituted solely by the human labour contained in them.[2] If anyone defined the value of a thing as the amount of human labour in it, this would be a very bad guide to the price that people actually pay for it, or to the amount that they actually esteem it in their hearts. It is easy to find two things A and B such that A takes less labour to produce than B and yet commands a higher price than B. And it is easy to find two things C and D such that C takes less labour to produce than D and yet is more esteemed and valued than D. Why then is a labour-definition of value attractive? Because it is not really an attempt to describe facts at all, but the expression of a moral ideal. It is Marx's moral demand that the products of labour shall all go to the labourers, and this arouses some response in every heart.

However, Marx presents his moral demand as if it were a statement of fact, with an immense apparatus of quantitative details and economic terminology. This eighth form of real definition is a moral or evaluative appeal misrepresented as a statement of fact, and gaining force from its pseudo-scientific character. The general pattern of this, namely, exhortation and appeal and moral judgement masquerading as science, is more than usually common in Marxism.

Leo Tolstoy asked 'What is art?', and pursued the question through an essay of twenty chapters, passionately developing and enforcing the answer that true art is the communication of universal or religious feelings. Now as an account of what is ordinarily meant by the word 'art', or as an analysis of the thing ordinarily referred to by the word, Tolstoy's answer is absurd. It is perfectly evident that a vast amount of art is not the communication either of a universal or of a religious feeling. Tolstoy himself makes this evident by calling to his readers' minds a great many well known works of art, such as Wagner's operas and Baudelaire's verses, and saying that

[1] *Plato today*, New York, 1939, p. 303.   [2] *Capital*, I ch. I.

they are not art. He even says that only two of his own writings are art, namely, the short stories *A Prisoner of the Caucasus* and *God Sees the Truth but waits*; whereas it is obvious that his novels *Anna Karenina* and *War and Peace* are also art.

What led Tolstoy into these amazing statements is the fact that the word 'art', besides having a definite descriptive function, also has a fairly strong evaluative function. To call a thing 'a work of art' is not always merely to describe it as belonging in the class of, say, statues, and not in the class of animals; it is often also to *evaluate* it as beautiful and pleasing to the senses and desirable. Tolstoy came to value the set of things commonly described as 'art' differently from the way most people value them. He came to feel that they were all bad, not good, except those that communicated universal or religious emotions. He wished to make us feel so too. He wished to transvaluate our aesthetic values, to adapt a phrase from Nietzsche. His method of doing so was to direct the favourable emotional power of the word 'art' away from all the works of art he disapproved, by denying that they were art and defining art as the thing that he approved.

Mr. T. S. Eliot in his *Notes towards a Definition of Culture* (1948) appears to be concerned mainly to put forward a persuasive definition of culture, or to prepare the ground for one. Although he refers often to the anthropologists' use of the word 'culture', which is not evaluative but purely descriptive, his purpose appears to be not to analyse what the anthropologists mean by the word, but to decide which possible type of culture (in the anthropologists' sense) he is prepared to adopt and recommend as the ideal towards which we should move.

This peculiar sort of real definition was first described, so far as I know, by Professor C. L. Stevenson, and can be found brilliantly set out in his book *Ethics and Language*. He calls it 'persuasive definition'. He points out that persuasive definitions often use the words 'true' or 'real'. 'True *x* is *yz*.' Persuasive definitions aim at altering the descriptive meaning of a term without altering its emotional meaning, thus directing the emotion towards a new object. One who prefers dash to prudence may say that true courage is never feeling the emotion of fear. One who prefers prudence to dash may say that true courage is persisting with rational purposes in spite of the solicitations of fear. Each is recommending his ideal of human behaviour in respect of fear.

An essentially similar procedure is often carried out by means of the word 'function' instead of the word 'definition'. Sentences of the form 'the function of x is y' profess to be statements of fact. Sometimes they are, e.g. 'the function of a porous flowerpot is to get rid of excessive water'. But sometimes they are not, e.g. 'the function of poetry is not to give pleasure, to disseminate knowledge, or to promote character'. It is certain that hundreds of persons have written what they called 'poetry' with the intention of giving pleasure, and hundreds with the intention of disseminating knowledge, and hundreds with the intention of promoting character. If, therefore, we take this sentence as a universal statement of fact, it is absurdly false. It is in reality a means by which the writer expresses and enforces his wish that verse shall not be used to give pleasure, &c., but for some other purpose which he is going on to tell us. He hopes to succeed by persuading us to refuse the high name of 'poetry' to many things to which it has been applied in the past. A. E. Housman's lecture on *The Name and Nature of Poetry* largely consists in such a manipulation of the word 'poetry' in the service of a particular allegiance. Sentences saying that 'the function of man is A' are either attempts to persuade us to devote ourselves to A, or else the writer thinks he knows that some superbeing, either Nature or God, made men for a particular purpose, just as men make hammers to drive home nails.

What is the value of persuasive definition? The habit of evaluating things is presumably ineradicable from human nature, and certainly desirable. The habit of trying to get other persons to share our own valuations is equally ineradicable and equally legitimate. What is hard to decide is whether persuasive definition is a desirable way of trying to change people's opinions. The argument against it is that it involves error and perhaps also deceit. The only persons who are influenced by a persuasive definition, it may be said, are those who do not realize its true nature, but take it to be what every real definition professes to be, a description of the objective nature of things. A persuasive definition, it may be urged, is at best a mistake and at worst a lie, because it consists in getting someone to alter his valuations under the false impression that he is not altering his valuations but correcting his knowledge of the facts. I am tentatively inclined to accept this view, with the practical conclusion that we should not use persuasive definitions. But the whole question of what methods of moral persuasion are moral must be re-examined from the beginning, in the light of the new doctrine that ethical language is not descriptive but evaluative.

If we decide that persuasive definitions are necessarily deceptions and therefore should not be used, it follows that they should not be called 'real definitions'; for if we called them so we should certainly tend to suggest the falsehood that they were descriptions of fact. Tolstoy should not have said that he was 'defining' art, nor should we say that Plato 'defines' justice in the *Republic*.

§ 9. **Real Definition as Abstraction.** Ninthly, the search for real definitions has very often been a search for analyses.

But what is analysis? This word is used in more than one sense. I shall try now to describe some of the activities which the word 'analysis' is used to mean, and to say which of them are ever intended by the phrase 'real definition'.

The first sense of 'analysis' which I shall mention is *abstraction*. Abstraction is becoming aware for the first time of a new general element in one's experience and giving it a name. A general element is a form or pattern or characteristic, as opposed to a particular or individual. To become aware of a particular cow in a field is not called 'abstraction'. But it is called 'abstraction' to become aware of the form cow as opposed to the form bull or the form sheep. It is not abstraction to become aware of a particular bright colour somewhere in one's field of vision, but it is so to become aware of rose as a form distinct from other colours. In 1942 many persons became aware for the first time of physiological shock, by studying the U.S. manual of first aid. In reading the account of shock they realized that they had formerly seen shock in others or in themselves, but had not recognized and named it as a special pattern of its own. They had not, until they read the book, abstracted it from the complex mass of their experience.

When one thus becomes aware for the first time of a new common element of experience, one may or may not recall having experienced it in the past. Some of those who read about shock recognized that they had previously experienced shock, though without distinguishing it from the mass of other experience in which it was embedded, that is, without abstracting it. Others recalled no such experience. I will call all new awareness of a general form in experience 'abstraction', whether or not the abstractor recognizes the form as having occurred without abstraction in his previous experience. (But in common speech we have some tendency to confine the word to cases where we do recall previous occurrences of the form, unrecognized as such at the time.)

The symbolic activity that expresses and confirms abstraction is naming. When the physiologist gives the name 'shock' to a form observed in the behaviour of the body, or the psychologist gives the name 'closure' to a phenomenon recognized in perception, or the critic gives the name 'poetry' to a form observed to be present both in epics and lyrics and novels and plays but absent from histories and cookbooks, they record and strengthen their awareness of a certain character recurrent in their experience.

This first sort of analysis, namely, abstraction, is sometimes called 'definition', and therefore constitutes my ninth kind of real definition. Thus Cook Wilson writes of 'the formation . . . of a definition by abstraction of a universal from particulars'.[1] It is, of course, a genuine and most valuable and extremely common activity of the human mind. But it is certainly not one that ought to be called 'definition'. The proper names for it are 'abstraction' and, when we are thinking of its symbolic side, 'naming'. People call it 'definition' only when they confuse it with another kind of analysis, to which I now turn.

§ 10. Real Definition as Analysis. The second kind of analysis, which I will now try to describe, is a mental process which forms the next stage after abstraction. It is the process of analysing a general element after it has been abstracted

[1] *Statement and Inference*, I 378, cf. 28.

and named. We sometimes do not rest satisfied with having abstracted a new form, but desire to analyse it. The first-aid book says: 'An immense amount of experimental work has failed to show exactly what happens in shock.' A psychologist writing on 'The Metaphor of Closure' in the *Psychological Review* for 1941 takes the position that, while everyone intuitively recognizes closure in perception, no one defines it, and we ought to have a definition of it, that is, an analysis. When a thinker asks what is religion, or what is obscenity (as D. H. Lawrence does in *Obscenity and Pornography*), or what is envy or any other emotion (as Spinoza does in *Ethics*, III), he is trying to proceed from the abstraction and naming of a form to the analysis and definition of it. What is the psychological difference between dreaming and waking? What is pastoral poetry?[1] The activity is immensely common.

The passage from abstraction to analysis was called by Leibniz the passage from having a clear idea to having a distinct idea. My idea of a thing is clear or vivid, he said, if I can recognize examples of the thing; but it is not distinct until I can also enumerate one by one the marks that distinguish this form from others.

This kind of analysis is the becoming aware of the complexity of the form, 'the exhibition of a given object', as W. E. Johnson put it, 'in the form of a synthesis of parts into a whole' (I 107). For it is possible to know a form that is complex without knowing its complexity; and it is possible later to come to know its complexity, and then to see that this complexity was always in the form that one knew, although at first one was not aware of it, or was aware only that probably the form was complex.

This occurs, for example, when the schoolchild learns that the circle, with whose name and nature he has been familiar in one way for years, is, though he never realized it before, the curve which is the locus of all the points in a plane equidistant from a given point. He is then analysing an object which he previously knew as an unanalysed whole. And such an event has often been referred to by the phrase 'real definition'.

[1] William Empson, *Some Versions of Pastoral*, e.g. p. 8.

Some might say that the above so-called process of 'real definition' is actually the process of substituting one nominal definition for another. Previously the child has used the word 'circle' to mean a certain perceptible shape. He is now told that, for the purposes of geometry, he must use and understand this word in a new sense. It is no longer to mean a perceptible shape, but simply and solely the curve of all points equidistant from a given point, even if such a figure should be for any reason necessarily imperceptible. There is thus no question of any analysis or real definition, but only of using an old word in a new sense, i.e. of replacing one nominal definition by another.

This line of thought, however, appears to go too far in its anxiety to condemn real definition. The replacement of one nominal definition by another is, of course, a common event; and no doubt this event has often occurred upon the occasion of someone's reading the geometer's definition of 'circle'. But sometimes something else occurs, either instead of or in addition to the substitution of one nominal definition for another. This other event is that some human soul for the first time realizes the possibility of there being a curve whose every point is equidistant from a given point, and for the first time realizes that such a curve is the perceptible circle which has long been familiar to him in many apparitions. This is an important event in the education of a human being; and we should avoid language which tends to conceal the occurrence of it, and to suggest that nothing more can possibly be happening than the substitution of one nominal definition for another. Such language is sometimes uttered by persons eager to maintain that real definition is a muddle.

The doctrine that stipulation is free, besides having the defects which I described in Chapter IV, is liable to make us overlook the sort of analysis here mentioned. When we ask what the thing x is, believing it to be analysable but not possessing the analysis, a certain type of person replies, 'you are free to make the word "x" mean anything you like', as if there were nothing at issue but a choice of nomenclature. There is at issue, however, the achievement of an increased insight into the nature of some thing.

There is probably a converse process to this kind of analysis, the process of losing sight of the complexity of a complex form, of going back, or going for the first time, to the state of apprehending it as an unanalysed whole. But this is not what is usually meant by the word 'synthesis', which is thought to name the converse of analysis. By the word 'synthesis' is usually meant the process of apprehending a new complex form in its complexity by mentally constructing it out of its elements.

Evidently a form which was not complex could never be analysed in the above sense of 'analysis'. If any forms are simple, they are unanalysable. And if any forms are unanalysable, they are indefinable so far as by 'definition' we mean analysis. And this is the point that men have mostly been aiming at when they asserted that some things are indefinable. And here if anywhere is the justification for the belief in indefinability. There is no justification for believing in indefinable *words*; but there is for believing in indefinable *forms* if and only if some forms are simple. However, no conclusive reason for believing in the occurrence of absolute simplicity has yet been found. Some have argued that 'if there are complexes there must be simples'. But the existence of complexes necessitates only the existence of relatively simple things, not also of absolutely simple things.

I should say that this kind of analysis is what Professor Moore had in mind when he wrote in *Principia Ethica* that good and yellow are indefinables. 'The most important sense of "definition"', he there wrote, 'is that in which a definition states what are the parts which invariably compose a certain whole' (9); and 'we cannot define anything except by an analysis' (10). The first chapter of this book contains much elucidation of the conception of real definition as analysis. I cannot reconcile this, however, with Professor Moore's writing in *The Philosophy of G. E. Moore*, p. 663, that he meant by 'giving an analysis' of a concept a process such that 'nobody can know that the *analysandum* applies to an object without knowing that the *analysans* applies to it'. For it seems to me that if this were true there would never be any difficulty in analysing anything. Everyone who knew that here was a case of humility would know the analysis of humility; and everyone who knew that the number of fractions is infinite would know the analysis of infinity. But this second kind of analysis is patently an insight that is often very difficult to attain, and not given to everyone who is aware of the *analysandum*. Many things have never been analysed to the satisfaction of all, such as sin, love, humility, obscenity, humanism, romanticism. And though this may be in some cases because the thing is not complex, and in other cases because the supposed thing is really a bundle of things held together by nothing better than an ambiguous word, it seems overwhelmingly probable that there remain cases in which analysis is possible but not yet achieved. It seems evident, moreover, that certain forms which are now convincingly analysed were at certain past times not analysed, although men had been trying to analyse them; for examples, infinity, force.

The same peculiar view that analysis is always easy and obvious seems to be implied in Sir David Ross's statement: 'The fact that we use the term "good" intelligently and intelligibly without having any definition of it in our minds shows that it is indefinable.'[1]

The difficulty of this kind of analysis is connected with the fact that there is no mechanical method for performing it. Like artistic creation and scientific theorizing, it is a groping affair. It is usually a matter of hypothesis and verification. We have to conceive hypotheses as to the analysis of our form, and then we have to test them. There is no sure method of conceiving hypotheses, as there is no sure method of getting ideas of any sort. And there is no sure method of testing them once conceived. Occasionally we feel a strong intuitive confidence that a proposed analysis is correct; but it is sometimes incorrect nevertheless. The sort of way in which analysing must proceed is the aporematic, groping method often illustrated in Aristotle's writings, collecting suggestions, considering objections to them, calling up all relevant observations, and finally making a judgement. Kant said that an *a-priori* concept as given contains many obscure ideas which we may overlook in analysing it; hence we can never be demonstratively certain that our analysis of it is

[1] *The Right and the Good*, p. 92.

complete. In general, his view[1] seems to be that analysis can never be certain except in the trivial case where it is merely taking apart what I have myself explicitly and consciously put together.

The occurrence of this kind of analysis is a paradox to many of us. It seems absurd that we should know a complex form and yet not know its complexity. For what is the form, we argue, except a certain complex of certain elements? Therefore, if we know the form we know the complex. Or we may state the paradox with reference to the verbal expression of an analysis thus: If the *analysans* means the same as the *analysandum*, the expression is trivial; while, if it means something different, the expression is false.

But it would, in my judgement, be a mistake to let this paradox persuade us that after all analysis as described above does not really occur, and the experiences that seem to be analyses must be explained away. An experience conscientiously described is more worthy of belief than a dialectical dilemma. I am not even sure that it is worth investigating why we are so astonished at the fact of analysis. Many indubitable propositions are perpetually astonishing to many of us, for example that there are just as many odd integers as there are integers altogether, or that between any two points on a line there are others, or that, although 3 is half-way from 2 to 4, 1/3 is not half-way from 1/2 to 1/4. No one nowadays thinks it worth investigating why the Pythagoreans were amazed at the incommensurability of the diagonal.

This second kind of analysis (probably the commonest of all logical meanings of the word) has very often been what was meant by the phrase 'real definition'; and this is already clear from my description of it, in which I have had to quote passages, especially from *Principia Ethica*, where it is explicitly called 'definition'. Just as the symbolic activity which expresses and confirms the act of abstraction is naming, so, we may say, the symbolic activity which expresses and confirms the act of analysis is definition. This sort of analysis constitutes, therefore, my tenth sort of real definition. Correspondingly, the word 'indefinable' has frequently meant unanalysable in this sense.

---

[1] In *Critique of Pure Reason*, A 728–30.

What is its value? My answer to this question is clearly implied in the above descriptions of it. It is a genuine and most important form of insight.

Should we continue to call it 'real definition' in future? That is a hard decision to make. In favour of doing so is the fact that it is precisely the thing that the phrase 'real definition' has most of all been used to mean in the past. There is also the question what else we can call it if we do not call it 'real definition'. The only obvious alternative is 'analysis', and that has its own disadvantage, namely, it is itself a highly ambiguous word. I have already shown that it has at least two senses; and I shall introduce several more in what follows. A third consideration, in favour of continuing to call it 'real definition', is that, whatever decision we logicians may make, it is certain that hosts of laymen will go on calling this activity 'definition'; and perhaps it would be better for us to follow common usage.

Against continuing to call this activity 'real definition', on the other hand, stands the fact that this phrase indicates even less of its nature than the word 'analysis' does. Furthermore, this phrase invites us to confuse it with all the other things that have also been called 'real definition'. And one of these confusions is immensely common and immensely harmful. The failure to distinguish all the time between the analysis of things and the nominal definition of words has been the cause of most of the common errors in the theory of definition. It is the cause of people's having believed all the following false propositions:

1. The definition of words must always proceed by analysis, or by genus and differentia, or the like.
2. The definition of a word must never contain any term synonymous with the word being defined.
3. Proper names are indefinable.
4. Names like 'red', 'sour', 'loud', are indefinable.
5. Some words must be indefinable because otherwise there would be either an infinite regress or a circle.
6. A definition is an equivalence.
7. There is essence.

This confusion is also the cause of a great deal of that confused language which attributes meaning to things that are not symbols. Here is an example of such language from a recent issue of a philosophical journal: 'Ultimates which we cannot fully and exhaustively define, but which nevertheless have meaning.' The only things that have meaning are words and other symbols; and all symbols can be defined. I think we can confidently say that the confusion between the analysis of things and the nominal definition of words has been by far the most damaging error in the theory of definition, and among the most damaging errors in the whole of philosophy.

When I attempt to weigh these considerations *pro* and *contra*, I find myself judging, though very tentatively, that we had better give up calling this activity 'definition' or 'real definition' in future, and call it 'analysis'. Correspondingly, we had better give up talking of 'indefinability', and call it 'unanalysability' instead.

§ 11. **Real Definition as Synthesis.** In the third place, peculiar as it seems, there is little doubt that the word 'analysis' is often used to mean the opposite of analysis, namely, synthesis. If *a* and *b* together compose the complex *c*, and *c* in turn is part of the bigger complex *d*, then the process of realizing that *c* is a complex of *a* and *b* is what I call 'the analysis of *c*', and the process of realizing that *c* is an element in the bigger complex *d* is something that I should not call 'an analysis of *c*', but 'an analysis of *d*', or possibly 'a synthesis of *c* into the larger whole *d*'. Both these processes have, however, frequently been called 'analyses of *c*'. Thus what is called in cricket the 'bowling analysis', and what is often meant in statistical inquiries by 'analysing the data', are processes of synthesizing a great many details into a few generalizations. And this curious usage is almost deliberately adopted by C. I. Lewis when he writes that 'logical analysis is not dissection but relation', and that 'the comparison of terms to points in a spatial pattern, and of definitions to the tracing out of such patterns of relationship, is much more apt than that other metaphor which represents logical analysis as physical dissection'.[1] This is a good statement of the fact that many people have meant by the phrase 'analysing *x*' something like integrating *x* into some larger

[1] *Mind and the World Order*, pp. 82, 106.

whole. Whereas 'analysis' originally meant something like the exhibition of an object as a synthesis of parts into a whole (W. E. Johnson), it nowadays often means something like the exhibition of an object as a part which is synthesized into some larger whole.

This third kind of analysis, namely, synthesis, constitutes an eleventh activity that has often been covered by the name 'real definition'. The so-called 'definition' of a concept or a form has frequently been the discovery of its place in a system of concepts or forms. Especially has this been so in mathematical or logical systems, where various concepts have been 'analysed into', or 'defined in terms of', the primitive concepts. When a man says 'I define other men's emotions in terms of my own sensations', he usually does not mean analysis in the sense of revealing the complexity of other men's emotions, for that would make him a solipsist; he would be saying that his wife's laughter is nothing but a certain pattern of a certain set of his own sensations. But he means analysis in the sense of synthesizing other men's emotions into a large whole which includes also his own sensations, and locating them within that whole by reference to his own sensations. The same thing is implied in phrases like 'terrestrial longitude is defined in terms of Greenwich'. This does not mean that Greenwich or the longitude of Greenwich is a constituent in any other place, but merely that we make use of Greenwich as a point of reference for indicating any point in the system of longitudes which synthesizes all places. And where definition merges into classification, as in the taxonomy of the forms of life, we have another case of synthesis, of perceiving the place of the thing 'defined' or classified in a larger system.

Evidently such synthesis is a valuable activity whenever it is true. But should we call it 'analysis' and should we call it 'real definition'? The answer seems to be that we should avoid calling it by either of these names whenever we can, but it is not clear whether we always can, and only a great deal of collecting and examining usages would make it clear. One of the main reasons why it has been called 'analysis' probably is that we need a single word as a name for the generic activity of either analysing or synthesizing, and one of the two specific names had to serve for this purpose also, and 'analysis' was chosen because it is the more pronounceable word and because analysis is the more obvious of the two species. Having thus come to mean the generic activity of either analysing or synthesizing, the word 'analysis' could more easily go on to mean the other species, namely, synthesis. The phrase 'is defined in terms of' can usually be profitably replaced by some such phrase as 'is referred to' or 'is located by reference to'.

§ 12. **Real Definition as the Improvement of Concepts.** The original metaphor of analysis was that of taking apart pieces that had been put together into a whole. Penelope promised her importunate suitors that she would choose one of them when she had finished the cloth she was weaving; but every night she secretly 'analysed' what she had 'synthesized' during the day. The three senses of 'analysis' so far described all preserve some connexion with this original metaphor. The second sense, discovering the complexity of a complex, is the closest. The first, namely, abstraction, is a process that leads to the second. The third, synthesis, is the reverse of the second. But the word is often used in senses that retain no trace of the original notion of undoing. The first three senses are all cases of reflection, or processes of thinking or knowing in which reflection predominates and perception plays little or no part. And the word is often extended to mean other sorts of reflection, although they do not suggest the original analogy. This is a common pattern in the biography of words, well illustrated in Ogden and Richards's *Meaning of Meaning*. Because it means *A* a word is later applied to *B*, and because *B* is a *C* the word comes to be applied to other *C*'s in which there is no trace of *A*.

The most important of these advanced senses of the word 'analysis', from which the original metaphor has wholly disappeared, is perhaps the improvement of our ideas. To 'analyse' a concept sometimes means to improve it, that is, to substitute for it a very similar concept which is superior. Since by 'real definition' is sometimes meant this fourth kind of analysis, we have here a twelfth sort of real definition. This sort of definition is not analysis (in the strict sense, i.e. the second sense) but substitution. In this sense to ask

'What really is piety?' is equivalent to saying: 'My old concept of piety is not good enough any more; I want a more precise (or penetrating, or comprehensive) insight into the range of reality to which the word "piety" has pointed.' Just as when we speak of 'formulating the question' we really mean replacing our present question by a similar but better one, so when we speak of 'defining' a thing we sometimes mean replacing our conception by a better one.

When is a concept improved? What makes one concept better than another very similar one?

It is often thought that a concept is improved by being made *more general*. On this view, for example, each of the following concepts would be an improvement on the preceding:

1. A cylinder is the solid generated by a circular area moving along a straight line passing through the area at right angles.

2. A cylinder is the solid generated by any area moving along a straight line passing through the area at right angles.

3. A cylinder is the solid generated by any area moving along a straight line passing through the area at any constant angle.

It cannot, however, be true for all purposes that a concept is improved by being made more general; for, if it were so, then, after improving all our concepts as much as possible, we should have no specific concepts left. For example, we should have no concept of robin as opposed to bird, since bird is a concept very similar to robin but more general. Other things being equal, generality is a loss as well as a gain. The generalization of the concept of *x* is a pure improvement of it when all the main things we are accustomed to say about *x* according to our old concept of it are also true of it according to our new concept of it. But on other occasions we may improve the concept of *x* by narrowing it, namely, when the things we believe about *x* are false of it according to our earlier, general concept, but true of it according to our later, specific concept. In § 3 of my chapter on word-thing definition I have generalized the concept of word-thing definition, mainly on the ground that there is no important difference between those cases of teaching the meaning of a word that have in the past been called 'definition' and those that have not. Thus I urged that the things we habitually said about word-thing definition according to our old concept of it were true also of other things, and therefore our concept of word-thing definition ought to be generalized so as to make what we say about it commensurate with it.

A second suggestion about the improvement of concepts is that we improve a concept if it is selfcontradictory and we substitute for it a similar concept that is selfconsistent. Here everyone would agree that such a procedure would always be an improvement; but some might doubt whether it ever occurs, on the ground that concepts are never self-contradictory. But the following are surely selfcontradictory concepts:

1. The concept of the 'horned angle', i.e. the angle formed by the intersection of curved lines, this being distinct from any angle formed by the intersection of straight lines.

2. The concept of the regular decahedron, i.e. the solid whose sides are ten regular polygons of identical size and shape (Leibniz's example).

3. The concept of justice as such a distribution of scarce goods that everybody has as much as he needs and deserves and wants.

Selfcontradictoriness in a concept is a species of a larger defect that perhaps most of our concepts have, the defect of including irrelevancies or false entailments and hence imputing to the experiences to which they are applied more than is actually experienced. The story of the man going round the squirrel that always faces him shows that our concept of going round includes the false idea that moving so as to be successively at all directions from an object entails moving so as to see successively all sides of that object. As Bridgman put it, there is in many of our terms a demand which perhaps reality cannot satisfy, but which we are usually convinced reality does satisfy, if we could only see how. Our concept of death, for example, is perhaps a demand that there shall be for all organisms a single very brief physiological event of identical character, such that for all times from its birth down to this event the organism is alive, while for all times after this event it is dead; and probably there is no such event. It is an improvement of a concept, therefore, to substitute for it a similar concept including fewer false entailments or demands that reality does not satisfy. Our early concept of downness demands absolute directions in space; since there are none such, it is an improvement to substitute for it the concept of downness as direction towards some given centre of gravity. The operations which build up a concept, wrote Bridgman, are often such that we have no right to the expectations which we have of that concept.[1]

In the fourth place, a concept appears to be usually improved if it is altered so that whether or not it applies to a given event is more easily determined. Einstein is said to have defined simultaneity so that it became theoretically possible to say of any two events whatever whether they were simultaneous, which it had not been before. And the theory of 'operational definition' developed from Einstein's procedure by Bridgman is, in part at any rate, a demand that we replace our concepts with similar concepts whose applicability can be always easily and unanimously determined by simple operations. When does a man die? When his heart stops beating? But suppose it starts again an hour later? When his heart stops beating, never to start again? But then we can tell whether he has died only by waiting to see whether his heart does start again. If two hours later his heart has not started again, then he died two hours before; if it has, he did not. It seems most unsuitable that a man should be dead or alive now merely in virtue of what happens two hours later; and a revision of the concept of death which enabled us to apply it more precisely would be an improvement. Our use in practice of the concept of 'being pronounced dead by a doctor', in preference to the concept of 'being dead', shows how unserviceable the latter is in its actual condition.

The applicability of a concept has several sides. The one which I have so far brought out is that there must be something such as the concept applies to. Another is that the method of determining whether the concept applies to a given example should be as easy as possible; this is part

[1] *Philosophy of Science*, 1938, p. 128.

of Bridgman's reason for defining concepts by simple operations. Length should be defined in terms of simple operations like noting the coincidence of two rods or the simultaneity of two flashes. Another is that the method should give answers as nearly identical as possible whoever employs it. A fourth is that the borderland between the cases to which the concept applies and those to which it does not apply should be as narrow as possible, in other words, that the concept should be as precise as possible. To use an example brought forward by Professor Langford, our ordinary conception of an isosceles triangle does not tell us whether an equilateral triangle is isosceles or not. We improve it by defining 'isosceles triangle' so as to settle this point of application.

On the other hand, precision, like generality, is not always an improvement in a concept. It is good that we have our vague concepts of few and many as well as our precise concepts of one, two, three, &c. Otherwise we should be unable to give a friend any idea of how many people attended a meeting except by counting the precise number. One great advantage of precise concepts is that they make inference from statements containing them much safer. This, for example, is the reason for replacing the ostensive definition of the circle by an analytical definition.

Furthermore, this rule of applicability does not apply to ethical concepts. Bridgman and many other thinkers have been inclined to demand that we shall define or redefine our ethical concepts also in such a way that everyone can easily determine, in complete agreement with everyone else, what is a 'fair' wage, and whether euthanasia is 'wrong', and so on. But in using an ethical concept we are not describing the world but taking an attitude towards it. To call euthanasia wrong is to take up an attitude towards it, not to point out one of its characteristics or effects. A rational person will determine his attitude by means of his belief as to what the effects of permitting euthanasia would be; but still his attitude is distinct from his belief. And no definition can have the effect of making everyone take the same attitude to a given thing.

Concepts are improved, other things being equal, when

they are altered so as to fit into a system, or into a better or larger system. Thus the famous definition of implication in *Principia Mathematica*, '*p* implies *q* if and only if either *p* is false or *q* is true', while inconvenient in many respects, had the great advantage of building the notion of implication into a large and detailed system of ideas. This is a common purpose of definition in mathematics. And it is one of the few things about definition in mathematics that Pascal missed. 'Geometers impose names on things', he wrote, 'only in order to shorten their discourses, and not in order to diminish or alter the idea of the things they discourse about' (281). On the contrary, geometers and other mathematicians redefine common concepts to make them capable of entering into a system and yielding certain inferences. Thus what seemed to Pascal to be the nominal definition of a word is sometimes the real redefinition of a concept. Or, as Enriques put it, it is 'the use of nominal definitions as an expression of a process of conceptual construction'.[1] The error of mistaking the improvement of concepts for nominal definition is common among those who are sensitive to the confusions and illusions of real definition.

These various possible virtues of a concept, for the sake of which we may redefine it, are not easy to combine. There tends to be a conflict between those which the mathematician requires to make his system and those which the empiric requires to describe occurrences. The more precise a concept is, the more liable we are to be wrong in saying we have found a case of it in experience; but the less precise it is, the less we can use it in calculations.

If, as is held, empirical generalizations become definitions, this must involve definition as the improvement of concepts. This doctrine was put forward by Poincaré in *La Science et l'hypothèse*, and by Professor Lenzen in the *International Encyclopedia of Unified Science*, vol. I, part 5. A law which originates as a generalization from experience may, says Professor Lenzen, be transformed into a convention that expresses an implicit definition of the concepts it involves. I find his examples hard to follow, and cannot vouch for the correctness of the following attempt to reproduce two

[1] *The Historic Development of Logic*, p. 74.

of them. (1) Experience suggests that each successive oscil-lation of an undisturbed pendulum takes an equal amount of time. This may lead us to lay down as a law or postulate that each successive oscillation of an undisturbed pendulum must occupy an equal interval of time. But such a postulate is an implicit definition of the notion of equality in time. We may therefore revise our conception of equality in time, and say that by definition two periods of time are equal if and only if we can show that the ratio of their magnitudes is the same as the ratio of the times of two successive oscillations of an undisturbed pendulum. (2) Similarly, he suggests, the postulate that energy is never lost or gained leads to a redefi-nition of energy to conform with this postulate. For 'if in a physical process the total change of known forms of energy is not zero, a new kind of energy is assumed in order to preserve the principle'.

A person setting out to make an analysis of the second kind, that is, to discover the complexity of a complex thing, will often end by making an analysis of this fourth kind, that is, altering and improving his concept of the thing. White-head and Russell said in *Principia Mathematica* that, when what they define is something familiar, their definitions con-tain an analysis of a common idea (p. 12). But these analyses often turn out to be *alterations* of the common idea rather than revelations of its complexity, notably the definition of implication. Similarly, on the opening page of *The Principles of Mathematics*, Russell, after giving a surprising definition of mathematics, writes: 'The definition professes to be, not an arbitrary decision to use a common word in an uncommon signification, but rather a precise analysis of the ideas which, more or less unconsciously, are implied in the ordinary employment of the term.' I am inclined to think, however, that it is neither a mere stipulation of a new meaning for the word 'mathematics', nor an analysis of the common idea of mathematics, but an improvement of the common idea of mathematics and a consequent stipulation of a new sense for the word. More often than not, perhaps, when we try to analyse a thing, we come out with an analytical concept of a new thing rather than of the thing we started with, because the attempt to analyse leads us to see a defect in our old concept.

In many other ways also the various kinds of real definition that I am describing slide into each other in actual thinking. I do not suggest that every case of real definition in the past has fallen into one of my classes to the exclusion of all the others; but that in the future we shall fare better if we are aware which of these sorts of thinking we are engaged in at any given time.

Like the analysis (sense 2) of concepts, the improvement of concepts is often a very difficult and groping operation. One or both of these activities are what Frege seems to have had in mind in writing the following words: 'It often requires great intellectual work, which may take several centuries, to apprehend a concept in its purity, to extract it from the extraneous coverings that hid it from the eye of the mind.'[1]

Every improvement of a concept carries along with it a stipulative redefinition of the word expressing the concept. We have here, therefore, in this form of real definition, an activity in which real and nominal definition must both occur together. If, in attempting to analyse the thing art, a man is led to believe that his concept of art has been inadequate and to remake it, including perhaps history in art whereas he formerly excluded it, he is at the same time necessarily stipulating a new meaning for the word 'art'. Changes in insight lead to changes in nomenclature. Even the pure analysis of a concept, as opposed to its improvement, may lead to nominal redefinition; for, as Professor Langford points out, since the analysis gives us the thing as an explicit complex instead of as an apparent simple, we may decide in future to make the word mean the explicit complex instead of the apparent simple.

That this activity may be valuable is obvious; but should we call it 'analysis' and should we call it 'real definition'? Those who are strongly impressed by the mistakes liable to be insinuated by the word 'concept' will perhaps prefer either of these names to my name, 'the improvement of a concept'. But I incline to think that we must either use some such word as 'concept' or 'idea', or else prevent ourselves from saying many true and useful things. What is a concept? I suppose

[1] *Die Grundlagen der Arithmetik*, vii.

it is a habit, carried by a word, of thinking of a certain form, and usually also of thinking that this form is or may be realized somewhere. Some of our habits of thinking are habits of thinking *of* certain forms, rather than of certain other forms that we might think of instead. Such a habit, at any rate when it has a word to express and fix it, is a concept. Such a habit can certainly be altered and improved. It is better, because it leads to truer beliefs, to think habitually of and have names for some forms rather than others.

Here, as in the previous senses of 'analysis' and 'real definition', only a great study of usage could tell whether we can always get along satisfactorily without applying either of these terms to the improvement of concepts. But it seems desirable to do so whenever we can. The objections to calling it 'analysis' are at least as great as those to calling synthesis 'analysis'. The objections to calling it 'definition' are perhaps rather less, for the word 'definition' has always tended to carry an implication of alteration and improvement. But the liability to confusion with nominal definition remains.

So much for the fourth sense of 'analysis', which is the twelfth sense of 'real definition'. I do not know of any further senses of the word 'analysis' in which it means anything commonly included under the head of 'real definition'. But I will mention two of its other senses to distinguish them from the above.

The word 'analysis' is sometimes used, fifthly, to mean any activity of apprehending necessary truths, it being assumed that such truths are known by pure logic, without the aid of either experience or intuition or an *a-priori* synthetic function. Thus it is called an 'analytical' truth not merely that 'if p and q then p', but also that 'if p implies q then p and not-q are not both true'. In this wide sense analysis is the whole of the activity by which we come to know the truths of logic and mathematics, everything, that is, except the facts of history and their generalizations. This usage has come about in the following way. Certain propositions were called 'analytic' because, according to Kant, their truth was known by analysis (in the old sense of discovering the complexity of a whole), and not by experience or by any other means. Later some people came to think that all truths are known either by experience or by a process essentially the same as that by which we know Kant's analytic truth. All non-empirical truths were then said to be 'analytic'; but this analyticality was not thought to be necessarily being known by analysis in the old sense. Thus the word 'analysis', dragged along by the word 'analytic', tended to come to mean the process by which we know logic and mathematics, whatever that may be. It remains obscure, however, what this process is. For it is not 'analysis' in the old sense of resolving a complex, and 'analysis' in the new sense is merely a label.

Sixthly and lastly, there are many uses of the word 'analysis' in which it refers to some process that applies only to symbols, such as translating them into other symbols or discovering equivalent symbols; and all such processes must be distinct from my first four kinds of analysis, since these four apply to any complex object of thought, which need not be a symbol and usually is not. Most of the activities at Cambridge University that were called 'analysis' in the first half of the twentieth century were probably concerned only with symbols, and usually with compound symbols consisting of more than one word. Phrases like 'the author of *Waverley*', and sentences like 'I am a man', are typical examples of the objects of this analysis.

These last two kinds of analysis are never called 'real definition'.

§ 13. Conclusions about Real Definition. I conclude that the notion of real definition is a confusion of at least the following twelve activities:

1. Searching for an identical meaning in all the applications of an ambiguous word.
2. Searching for essences.
3. Describing a form and giving it a name.
4. Defining a word, while mistakenly thinking that one is not talking about words.
5. Apprehending a tautology determined by a nominal definition.
6. Searching for a cause.
7. Searching for a key that will explain a mass of facts.
8. Adopting and recommending ideals.

9. Abstracting, i.e. coming to realize a form.
10. Analysing, i.e. coming to realize that a certain form is a certain complex of forms.
11. Synthesizing, i.e. coming to realize that a certain form is a certain part of a certain complex form.
12. Improving one's concepts.

But why should so many activities have been confused under one name? A very large part of the cause of the birth and long life of this confused concept, real definition, is surely the occurrence in language, or at least in Indo-European languages, of the question-form: 'What is x?' Real definition first appears in literature as the answer to questions put by Socrates having the form 'What is x?' And the confusedness of the concept of real definition is an effect of the vagueness of the formula 'What is x?' For it is the vaguest of all forms of question except an inarticulate grunt.[1] Real definition flourishes because the question-form 'What-is-x?' flourishes; and this question-form flourishes precisely because it is vague. It saves us the trouble of thinking out and saying exactly what it is that we want to know about x. By saying 'What is x?' we can leave to our answerer the task of discovering what particular information about x we want. We can also use this question-form to express a general desire to be given any useful information about x of any sort.

(The question-form What-is-x? is even more ambiguous than the phrase 'real definition'; for, in addition to covering requests for all the activities that are ever called 'real definition', it also covers requests for other activities that are never so called. Thus 'Who is she?' may be a way of asking to be told a person's name, or her social status, or her profession, or her family relationship to some other person already known to the questioner.)

I conclude, secondly, that we had better drop the term 'real definition', and call each of the twelve different activities that 'real definition' has meant by a more specific name, and confine the term 'definition' to nominal definitions. There is nothing common to these twelve activities that calls for a common name. Nor do they form a system such as would

---

[1] This point is developed in the chapter on Socratic definition in my *Plato's Earlier Dialectic*, especially pp. 61–2.

justify applying the same term to each. The only system they form is the system of all the activities that have been muddled together under the name of 'definition'; and that deserves no common name. I propose then that by 'definition' we always mean a process concerning symbols, a process either of equating two symbols or of reporting or proposing a meaning for a symbol; and that we never use 'definition' as a name for a process that is not about symbols, because in that usage it is ambiguous and should be replaced by more specific terms.

Not, of course, that we shall ever be able to forget or ignore the term 'real definition' and the term 'definition' in the same sense. They are too central to the history of man's philosophical reflections and logical theories. They are ubiquitous and fundamental in the sources of Western philosophy, Plato and Aristotle. The concept of definition arose in the complex and confused form represented by the phrase 'real definition', not in the simple and clear form represented by the phrase 'nominal definition'. We shall have, therefore, constantly to use the term 'real definition' in referring to past literature and studying the history of thought. My suggestion is only that we should no longer use it in writing philosophy ourselves.

How can we avoid the phrases 'may be defined in terms of', &c.? We cannot change them all into 'may be analysed into a function of', &c., without losing the original metaphor of analysis. Since Whitehead and Russell took Not and Or as their two primitives, we are inclined to say that they analysed Equivalence as a function of Not and Or. But, since Lesniewski took Equivalence as his only primitive, we should then equally have to say that he analysed Not and Or as functions of Equivalence. But in the fullest sense of 'analysis' it is not possible that both x is in the analysis of y and y is in the analysis of x.

We can, however, say that 'Russell took Equivalence as a function of Or and Lesniewski took Or as a function of Equivalence'. The notion that both x is an unambiguous function of y and y is an unambiguous function of x is common and useful in the quantitative part of mathematics, and can, so far as I see, be extended to the logical part. Equivalence is $f_1(Or)$; but also Or is $f_2(Equivalence)$.

Ought we to abandon also the question-form 'What-is-x?' No; we need vague language as well as precise language. It is, however, useful that, when inclined to use the 'What-is-x?' form, we should consider whether a more definite form would be better. And it is very important that, when inclined to ask a question of this form, we should make sure that in our question the word 'x' has a proper meaning. There is no good in asking 'What is x?', meaning 'What is the thing x?', until the word 'x' means something to us, and means only one thing as opposed to many. There is no sense in saying that 'we don't know what x is' until we do know what the word 'x' means; for, if we did not know what the word 'x' meant, we should be uttering a meaningless noise in saying that 'we don't know what x is'.

VII

DEFINITION IN MATHEMATICS

I HAVE now completed the development of my theory of definition; and I propose to end by examining the role of definition in mathematics in the light of this theory.

In an axiomatized mathematical or logical system, such as is foreshadowed in Euclid's *Elements* and realized in many examples in the twentieth century, I find five or six different kinds of definition.

1. For the sake of *abbreviation* mathematicians introduce a new symbol and stipulate that it is to mean the same as a certain combination of old symbols. Thus 'i' is introduced as a conveniently short form to mean the same as the old phrase 'the square root of minus one'. Such a definition, being a stipulation, has no truthvalue. And, being merely an abbreviation, it is not a discovery and introduces no new idea, though the increased comprehension which it gives may help us to get new ideas in the future.

Abbreviation is a sort of aberrant case of original naming, aberrant because the name is related directly not to the nominand but to a phrase which describes the nominand; and what is primarily in the speaker's mind is not that this thing needs a name but that this thing needs a shorter name, or even that this phrase needs to be shortened.

Whitehead and Russell pointed out in *Principia Mathematica* that there is a clear sense in which such definitions are not really part of the system at all. The whole system could be written out without containing these definitions or the signs introduced by them. For example, we could strike out 'i' wherever it occurred and write '$\sqrt{-1}$' instead. The statement of the system would then take much longer, but contain the same ideas as before. 'Definition', they wrote, 'is not among the primitive ideas, because definitions are concerned solely with the symbolism, not with what is symbolised; they are introduced for practical convenience, and are theoretically unnecessary.'[1] In other words, if we use a certain

---

[1] *Principia Mathematica*, 2nd ed., p. 94, cf. p. 11.

symbolism in order to state a certain body of doctrine, then any remarks we have to make about the symbolism itself, before we can use it to state the doctrine, are not part of the doctrine. Similarly, oiling a bicycle is not part of using a bicycle, but a preparation for using it.

Whitehead and Russell also held, in *Principia Mathematica*, that this kind of definition is the only kind of definition occurring in mathematical systems. That is implied by their definition of 'definition' as 'a declaration that a certain newly introduced symbol or combination of symbols is to mean the same as a certain other combination of symbols of which the meaning is already known'. And it is the reason why they write as if not merely stipulative abbreviation but all definition were theoretically superfluous in mathematical systems. The view that abbreviation is the only form of definition in geometry also occurs in Pascal.

This view is quite untenable. It is perfectly evident that many definitions in mathematical systems are something other than stipulative abbreviations.

1. The symbol '⊃' is to mean the same as 'implies'.
2. 'p implies q' is equivalent to 'either p is false or q is true.' *Df.*

The first of these is an abbreviation, but the second is not. The first is useful but uninteresting; the second is very interesting, and has given rise to great discussion. It is not a 'mere typographical convenience'.[1] Its fundamental difference from the first is connected with the fact that, whereas the horseshoe means nothing before its definition, the word 'implies' means something before the second definition and continues to mean it afterwards.

2. Whitehead and Russell continue thus:

'In spite of the fact that definitions are theoretically superfluous, it is nevertheless true that they often convey more important information than is contained in the propositions in which they are used. This arises from two causes. First, a definition usually implies that the *definiens* is worthy of careful consideration. Hence the collection of definitions embodies our choice of subjects and our judgement as to what is most important. Secondly, when what is defined is (as often

---

[1] *Principia Mathematica*, p. 11.

occurs) something already familiar, such as cardinal or ordinal numbers, the definition contains an analysis of a common idea, and may therefore express a notable advance.'[1]

In this passage Whitehead and Russell are pointing to an important truth at the expense of contradicting themselves. In implying that the definiendum is an idea, as they do here, they contradict their definition of 'definition', according to which the definiendum is a symbol. And in saying that the definiendum is often 'something already familiar', they contradict their previous doctrine that the definiendum is by definition 'newly introduced'. Their previous doctrine must be abandoned and the present one retained; for a definition in mathematics is often a real definition in the sense of an *analysis* of an old idea. In other words, a definition in mathematics is often not a declaration that a certain new symbol is to mean the same as a certain combination of old symbols, but a statement of the discovery that a certain old symbol does mean the same as a certain combination of old symbols. Their definition, that 'p implies q' is equivalent to 'either p is false or q is true', was intended as an analysis of the old idea of implication, though subsequent discussion has shown that it is not the true analysis. This kind of definition is by no means external to the system.

3. Our first kind of definition in mathematical systems, namely, abbreviation, was relatively easy. The only difficulty in it is to find a sensible form having the conveniences required in a symbol, i.e. short yet distinct. Our second kind, the analysis of an idea, is hard. But the mathematician when he defines is often trying to do something harder still, namely, to analyse an idea in terms of a prescribed set of ideas. As Tarski has stated it, 'The question how a certain concept is to be defined is correctly formulated only if a list is given of the terms by means of which the required definition is to be constructed.'[2] The mathematician wants both to exhibit a certain form as a complex of other forms, and to insure that these other forms are all included in a certain set. He gives the names 'undefined ideas' and 'primitive ideas' to this set of forms to which he desires to reduce all other forms that he

---

[1] Ibid. pp. 11–12.

[2] *Logic, Semantics, Metamathematics*, p. 152.

mentions. Thus with regard to the concept of implication, both Whitehead and Russell in *Principia Mathematica*, and Lewis and Langford in *Symbolic Logic*, and Carnap in *Introduction to Semantics*, were trying not merely to analyse this concept but also to analyse it into some function of a specified set of concepts. This is usually the enterprise that is in the minds of logicians when they write of one thing as 'definable in terms of' others.

The mathematician furthermore desires to have his 'undefined' or 'primitive' concepts as few in number as possible, thus making things still more difficult for himself. Just as he wants to prove as many theorems as possible from as few axioms as possible, exactly so he wants to define as many concepts as possible from as few primitive concepts as possible. The two enterprises are parallel, as Tarski shows in *Logic, Semantics, Metamathematics*, pp. 296–319. Often, probably, the desire to reduce the number of primitive concepts is prior to the desire to analyse. Thus the twentieth-century attempt to analyse the concept of implication seems to have arisen not for its own sake but in order to construct a logic with as few primitive concepts as possible.

If an idea cannot be analysed into any function of a given set of primitive ideas, it is indefinable relative to that set. This is a perfectly real sort of indefinability, which mathematicians investigate with as much care as they investigate whether a certain proposition is 'decidable' on a certain set of postulates. But two points need to be remembered about this sort of indefinability. First, it is relative to a set of ideas; and an idea which is indefinable relative to one set of primitives may be definable relative to another. Second, it is an indefinability of ideas, not words. Though the idea of *x* may be indefinable as a function of the set of ideas, *a*, *b*, *c*, the word '*x*' is not for that reason indefinable. A word is never indefinable; that is to say, its meaning can always be explained to a suitable learner on a suitable occasion.

4. We have remarked, in considering 'real definition', that the thinker who sets out to analyse an idea often ends by improving the idea instead of analysing it. Much more often must this happen to a mathematical thinker who wishes not merely to analyse an idea but to do so in terms of a par-

ticular very small set of ideas. Consequently, a fourth sort of definition in mathematics is the *improvement of ideas*. In this case improvement consists primarily in substituting a new idea which, while covering the same or nearly the same set of particulars as the old, will reduce to the desired set of primitive ideas.

Such mathematical improvements or analyses of concepts often seem absurd to persons whose only conception of definition is teaching someone the meaning of a word he does not yet know, because they are often obscure, and when they are improvements instead of analyses they alter the meaning of the word. But they are not absurd; it is merely that the critic has mistaken their purpose; their aim is not to give people more vocabulary, but to create systems of concepts. Aristotle's definition of motion as 'the actualization of the potential in its potentiality' is a loose attempt to do the same kind of thing as the mathematician does rigorously. It is a reduction of the idea of motion to Aristotle's set of primitive ideas, namely, actuality, potentiality, form, matter, substance, &c. It is not bad merely because it is obscure, and could never teach a child the meaning of the word 'motion'; for that is not its intention.

5. The difference between the above kinds of mathematical definition and the ordinary nominal definition of words is emphasized by the fact that, to put it paradoxically, the undefined terms of a mathematical system are usually defined. To remove the paradox by putting in the qualifications, the terms which the systematizer uses to indicate his 'undefined' or 'primitive' concepts are usually informally defined by him in the course of his exposition, in order that his readers may know which concepts it is that he is making primitive. He often calls this 'informal definition'; and it is a kind of definition that lies 'outside the system' in a much truer sense than those which Whitehead and Russell called so. An example of it is the definition of the wedge sign in *Principia Mathematica*, p. 93: 'If p and q are any propositions, the proposition "p or q", i.e. "either p is true or q is true", where the alternatives are to be not mutually exclusive, will be represented by "$p \vee q$".' The authors say that this is not a definition but an explanation of this primitive idea. It

seems better to say that it is a pointing out of the idea and a nominal definition of their symbol for the idea.

In other words, the 'undefined ideas' of a system must have names; and these names must nearly always be defined, because they would otherwise be either completely unintelligible, like the wedge sign, or ambiguous, like the word 'or' in common speech. Hence we nearly always find, accompanying a statement of a mathematical system, nominal definitions of the names for the 'undefined' ideas.

Are such nominal definitions required only for the names of the primitive ideas, or also for the names of the derived ideas? The following consideration inclines us to answer that they are required only for the names of the primitive ideas. Since the derived ideas are all, in the course of the exposition, analysed into the primitive ideas, the statement of their analysis must serve also as an explanation of the meaning of the names for them. The analysis of the thing, and the definition of the name of the thing by the analytic method, are one and the same operation.

But this argument omits something important. In *Principia Mathematica* the horseshoe symbol stands for a derived idea. It is derived from the primitive ideas of negation and disjunction by the definition: $p \supset q. = .$ not–p or $q.Df.$ If the authors had left it at this, the above argument would apply to this case. The nominal definition of the horseshoe symbol would be given by the analysis of the horseshoe idea into a certain function of the primitive ideas of negation and disjunction. In fact, however, the authors did not leave it at that. They also coupled the horseshoe symbol with the word 'implies'. They made remarks which amounted to writing another definition of the horseshoe symbol, namely: $p \supset q. = . p$ implies q. And this was necessary if their formal definition was to contain, as they wrote, 'an analysis of a common idea'; for the horseshoe symbol without the word 'implies' would not have introduced any common idea to be analysed. It would have been absolutely nothing but a label for the idea of 'either p is false or q is true'. This consideration makes the following conclusion certain: if the formal definitions in a system are to give analyses or improvements of ideas, and not to be mere abbreviations, there must also be

informal definitions not merely of the primitive but also of
the derived ideas, or else the symbols for the derived ideas
must retain in the system a meaning which they have in
ordinary life. As Tarski has put it, 'there is no sense in discussing whether a term can be defined by means of other
terms before the meaning of those terms has been established'.[1]

6. Some definitions are said to be 'prescriptions for the
interpretation of calculi, by means of which formulae or parts
of formulae belonging to a calculus are coupled with objects
that are to be investigated through the calculus' (Dubislav).
Or, as Sigmund Koch puts what appears to be the same idea,
'coordinating definition correlates empirical constructs to the
formal terms of the postulate set, and thus transforms an
abstract system into an empirical one'.[2] This conception is
perhaps due to Professor Reichenbach, who discussed 'co-
ordinating definition' as early as 1920 in his *Relativitätstheorie und Erkenntnis A Priori*.

Are such interpretative definitions the same as our fifth
kind of definition in mathematical systems, the informal
definitions, or are they a sixth kind? I regret that I cannot
see clearly the answer to this. I can only put the question,
and hope that some mathematician will make the answer
plain to us. It demands a greater familiarity with examples
of the two sorts than I possess.

At present my hypothesis is that these so-called 'interpretative or co-ordinating' definitions are either the same as the
nominal definitions of the symbols of the system, which I
have treated in 5, or else a misnomer for the activity of pointing out examples to which the system applies.

I can explain what I mean by the possibility of their being
a misnomer thus. A series, according to Huntington in *The
Continuum*, is any class K, whose members are united by any
relation R, in accordance with all of the following four
postulates:

1. *Plurality*. The class K has more than one member.
2. *Connexity*. If a and b are distinct elements of K, then
   either aRb or bRa.

[1] *Logic, Semantics, Metamathematics*, p. 299 n.
[2] *Psychological Review*, XLVIII (1941) p. 21.

3. *Irreflexiveness.* If aRb, then a and b are distinct.

4. *Transitivity.* If aRb and bRc, then aRc.

Then we could offer, as an example of a series, the class of all points on a given line, say, one inch long, as united by the relation lying-to-the-left-of. Now perhaps someone would say that in doing this we are defining K as the class of all points on a given line; and defining R as lying-to-the-left-of; and that these were co-ordinating definitions. Then that would be an example of what I mean. It would be pointing to a case of K and miscalling that a definition of K. For the given postulates determine that the points on a line are a case of K and that many other sets are also. It is very probable, however, that this interpretation of 'co-ordinating definition' is mistaken.

I have now pointed out five or six kinds of definition that occur in mathematical systems, or at least in connexion with them:

1. *Abbreviations*, i.e. the introduction of a new term to mean the same as a certain complex of old terms.

2. *The analysis of concepts.*

3. *The analysis of concepts into specified concepts of the system.*

4. *The improvement of concepts*, especially their alteration so that they can be analysed into specified concepts of the system.

5. *The nominal definition of the symbols of the system,*

and perhaps also:

6. *Co-ordinating definition*, if this is both a genuine form of definition and distinct from the above. But I was not able to show that it is so.

Of these six kinds the second, third, and fourth belong to the complex of activities that have been confused together under the name of 'real definition'. The first, fifth, and sixth are nominal definitions. The fifth and sixth belong to the word-thing species of nominal definition. The first, perhaps, is sometimes word-thing and sometimes word-word.

Not all of the activities called 'definition' in mathematics are stipulative; this follows from the fact that some of them are not nominal definitions at all. But perhaps it is true that all the nominal definitions in mathematics are stipulative.

SOME DISCUSSIONS OF DEFINITION

ARISTOTLE, *Topics*, I 4–6, VI, VII 3; *Posterior Analytics*, I 2, 10, II 3–13; *Metaphysics*, Z 4–6, 10, 12, 15; *H* 3, 6.

BLACK, MAX, *Problems of Analysis*, pp. 3–37. Ithaca, New York, 1954

BRIDGMAN, P. W., *The Logic of Modern Physics*. New York, Macmillan, 1928. (Operational definition.)

— 'Operational Analysis', in *Philosophy of Science*, V (1938).

BROAD, C. D., *Examination of McTaggart's Philosophy*, I, c. vi. Cambridge, University Press, 1933.

CARNAP, RUDOLF, 'Testability and Meaning', *Philosophy of Science*, III, 1936.

CARROLL, LEWIS, *Through the Looking-glass*, c. vi.

COHEN, MORRIS, and NAGEL, ERNEST, *An Introduction to Logic and Scientific Method*, c. xii. New York, 1934.

DAVIDSON, WILLIAM L., *The Logic of Definition*. London, 1885. (Worthless.)

DUBISLAV, WALTER, *Die Definition*. Dritte Auflage. Leipzig, Felix Meiner, 1931. Beihefte der 'Erkenntnis', I.

DUBS, HOMER H., 'Definition and its Problems', in *Philosophical Review*, LII (1943).

ENRIQUES, FEDERIGO, *The Historic Development of Logic*. New York, 1929.

FREGE, GOTTLOB, *Translations from the Philosophical Writings of*, pp. 159–81, ed. Peter Geach and Max Black. Oxford, 1952.

GERGONNE, J. D., 'Essai sur la théorie des définitions', in *Annales de Mathématiques Pures et Appliqués*, IX (1818), pp. 1–35.

HOUSMAN, A. E., *The Name and Nature of Poetry*. Cambridge, University Press, 1933.

JOHNSON, SAMUEL, preface to the *Dictionary of the English Language*. London, 1755, &c.

JOHNSON, W. E., *Logic*, Part I, cc. vi, vii. Cambridge, University Press, 1921.

JOSEPH, H. W. B., *An Introduction to Logic*, 2nd ed., cc. iv–vi. Oxford, Clarendon Press, 1916.

KANT, IMMANUEL, *Critique of Pure Reason*, A 727–32.

KOCH, SIGMUND, 'The Logical Character of the Motivation Concept', in *Psychological Review*, XLVIII (1941).

LANGFORD, C. H., 'Moore's Notion of Analysis', in *The Philosophy of G. E. Moore*, ed. by P. A. Schilpp. Evanston, Illinois, 1942.

LEIBNIZ, G. W., 'Meditationes de Cognitione, Veritate, et Ideis', in *Opera Philosophica*, ed. J. E. Erdmann, 1840, pp. 79–81.

LENZEN, V. F., 'Procedures of Empirical Science'. *International Encyclopedia of Unified Science*, vol. I, part 5. Chicago, The University of Chicago Press, 1938.

LESNIEWSKI, STANISLAW, 'Über Definitionen in der sogenannten Theorie der Deduktion', *Comptes Rendus des Séances de la Société des Sciences et des Lettres de Varsovie*, XXIV, 1932. Classe iii.

LEVI, ALBERT WILLIAM, and FRYE, ALBERT MYRTON, *Rational Belief*, part i. New York, Harcourt Brace & Company, 1941.

LEWIS, C. I., *An Analysis of Knowledge and Valuation*, c. v. La Salle, Illinois, The Open Court Publishing Company, 1946.

— *Mind and the World-Order*. New York, Charles Scribner's Sons, 1929.

— 'Some Logical Considerations concerning the Mental', in *Journal of Philosophy*, XXXVIII (1941).

LOCKE, JOHN, *An Essay Concerning Human Understanding*, book iii.

MACKAYE, JAMES, *The Logic of Language*. Hanover, New Hampshire, Dartmouth College Publications, 1939.

MALONE, KEMP, 'On Defining *mahogany*', in *Language*, XVI 308.

MAUTHNER, FRITZ, *Beiträge zu einer Kritik der Sprache*, III 299–314. Stuttgart, 1901–2.

MILL, JOHN STUART, *A System of Logic*, introd. and I viii, IV iii–vi.

MOORE, G. E., *Principia Ethica*, c. i. Cambridge, University Press, 1903.

— 'A Reply to my Critics' in *The Philosophy of G. E. Moore*, pp. 660–7. Ed. P. A. Schilpp, Evanston, Illinois, 1942.

MORRIS, Charles W., 'Foundations of the Theory of Signs'. *International Encyclopedia of Unified Science*, vol. I, part 2. Chicago, The University of Chicago Press, 1938.

OGDEN, C. K., and RICHARDS, I. A., *The Meaning of Meaning*, c. vi. Fifth edition, London, 1938.

PASCAL, BLAISE, 'L'Esprit de la Géometrie', in *Pensées*, ed. Havet, 1881, vol. II.

PEPPER, S. C., *The Basis of Criticism in the Arts*, c. i. Cambridge, Massachusetts, 1945.

PLATO, *Euthyphro, Meno, Theaetetus* 146–8, 201–10, *Sophist, Statesman, Phaedrus, Letter* VII 342–4, *Laws*, X 895 DE.

POPPER, K. R., *The Open Society and its Enemies*, vol. II, c. xi, pp. 9–20. London, Routledge, 1945.

REICHENBACH, HANS, *Relativitätstheorie und Erkenntnis A Priori*. Berlin, Springer, 1920. (Chapter 3, 'Erkenntnis als Zuordnung', for co-ordinating definition.)

RICHARDS, I. A., *Interpretation in Teaching*. London, England, no date (1937?).

RICHARDS, I. A., and OGDEN, C. K., *The Meaning of Meaning*, c. vi. Fifth edition, London, 1938.

RICKERT, HEINRICH, *Zur Lehre von der Definition*, Freiburg i. B., 1888.

ROBINSON, RICHARD, *Plato's Earlier Dialectic*, c. v. Oxford, 1953.

RUSSELL, BERTRAND, *An Inquiry into Meaning and Truth*. New York, Norton, 1940.

— *Introduction to Mathematical Philosophy*, cc. i and ii. London, Allen & Unwin, 1919.

— and WHITEHEAD, A. N., *Principia Mathematica*, i. 11–12, 94. Second edition, Cambridge, University Press, 1925.

SCHLICK, MORITZ, *Allgemeine Erkenntnislehre*. Berlin, Springer, 1918. (Has a section on implicit definition.)

SCRIVEN, MICHAEL, 'Definitions, Explanations, and Theories', in *Minnesota Studies in the Philosophy of Science*, ed. Feigl, Scriven, and Maxwell, vol. II, 1958, pp. 98–195.

SEGERSTEDT, TORGNY, T., 'Some Notes on Definitions in Empirical Science', in *Uppsala Universitets Arsskrift 1957:2. Acta Universitatis Upsaliensis*.

SPINOZA, *Ethics*, I, prop. 8, n. 2; III end; and elsewhere.

— *Improvement of the Understanding*, second part.

STEBBING, L. S., *A Modern Introduction to Logic*, c. xxii. Second edition, London, Methuen, 1933.

STEVENSON, C. L., *Ethics and Language*, cc. ix, xiii. New Haven, Connecticut, 1944. Partly reprinted from *Mind*, XLVII (1938).

TARSKI, ALFRED, *Logic, Semantics, Metamathematics*, esp. pp. 296–319. Oxford, 1956.

— *Introduction to Logic and to the Methodology of the Deductive Sciences*. Enlarged and revised ed., New York, Oxford University Press, 1941.

— 'The Semantic Conception of Truth', in *Philosophy and Phenomenological Research*, IV (1943–4).

WHITEHEAD, A. N., and RUSSELL, BERTRAND, *Principia Mathematica*, I 11–12, 94. Second edition, Cambridge, University Press, 1925.

INDEX

Only topics for which there is no other obvious title are listed under the general head of 'Definition'.